Super-Dren

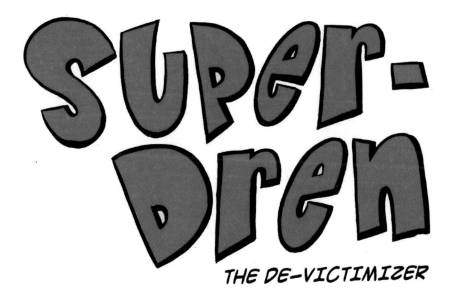

THE DE-VICTIMIZER

The Wisdom Pages
99 Wall St., Suite 1306
New York, NY 10005

For more information, visit **www.Bullies2Buddies.com**.

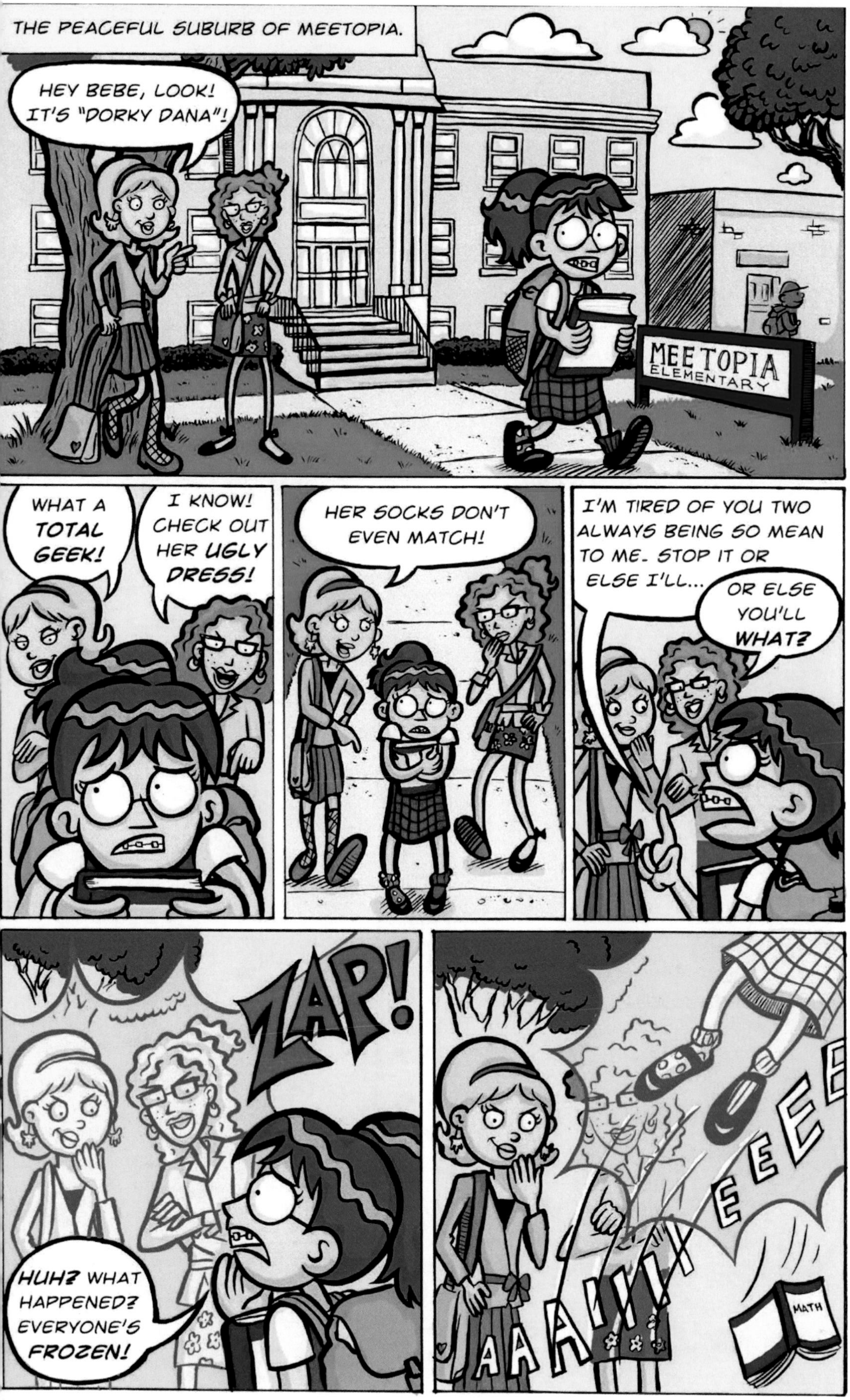
THE PEACEFUL SUBURB OF MEETOPIA.
HEY BEBE, LOOK! IT'S "DORKY DANA"!
MEETOPIA ELEMENTARY
WHAT A TOTAL GEEK!
I KNOW! CHECK OUT HER UGLY DRESS!
HER SOCKS DON'T EVEN MATCH!
I'M TIRED OF YOU TWO ALWAYS BEING SO MEAN TO ME. STOP IT OR ELSE I'LL...
OR ELSE YOU'LL WHAT?
ZAP!
HUH? WHAT HAPPENED? EVERYONE'S FROZEN!
AAAIIII EEEE
MATH

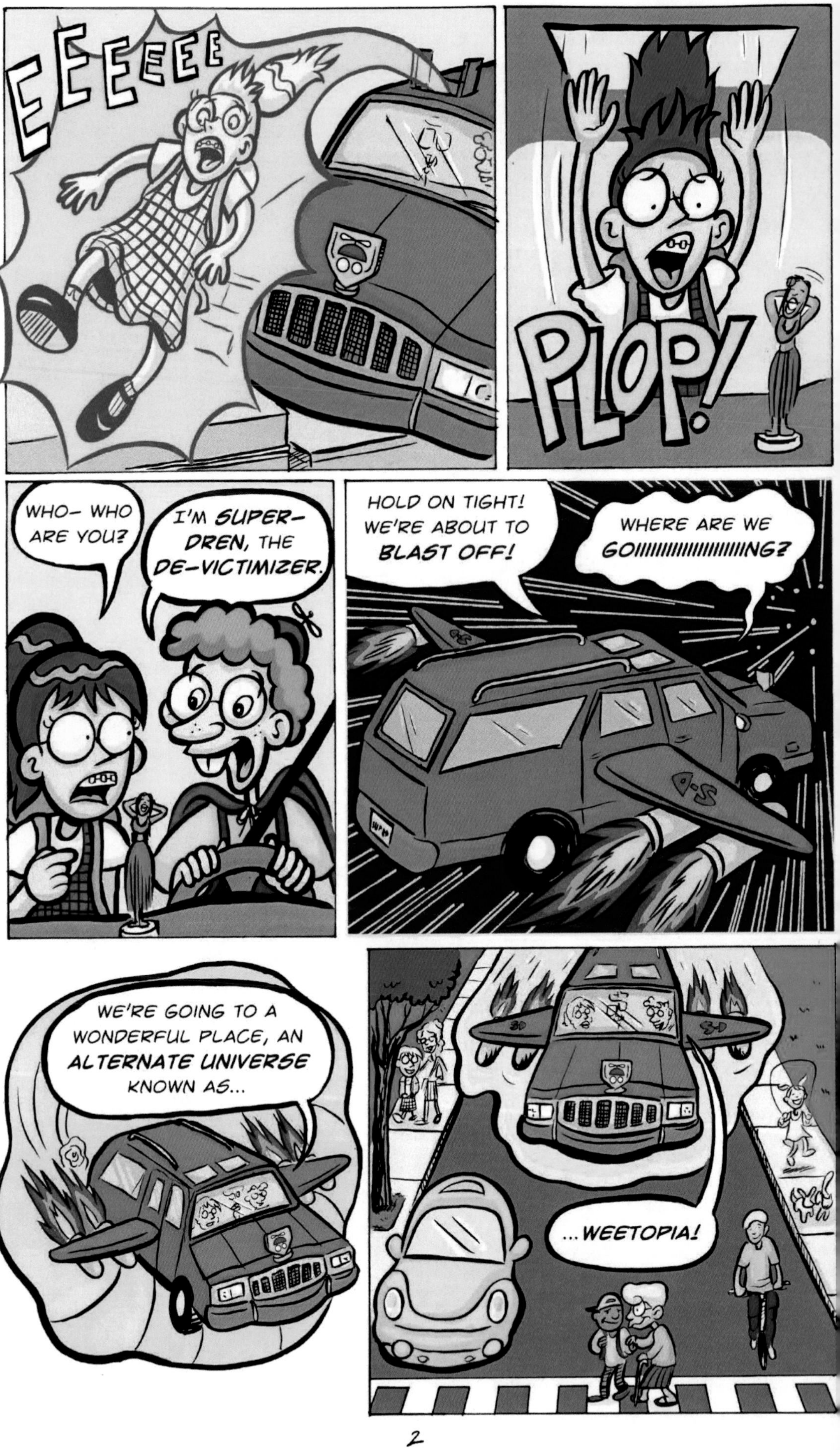
EEEEEE
PLOP!
WHO- WHO ARE YOU?
I'M SUPER-DREN, THE DE-VICTIMIZER.
HOLD ON TIGHT! WE'RE ABOUT TO BLAST OFF!
WHERE ARE WE GOIIIIIIIIIIIIIIIIIING?
WE'RE GOING TO A WONDERFUL PLACE, AN ALTERNATE UNIVERSE KNOWN AS...
...WEETOPIA!

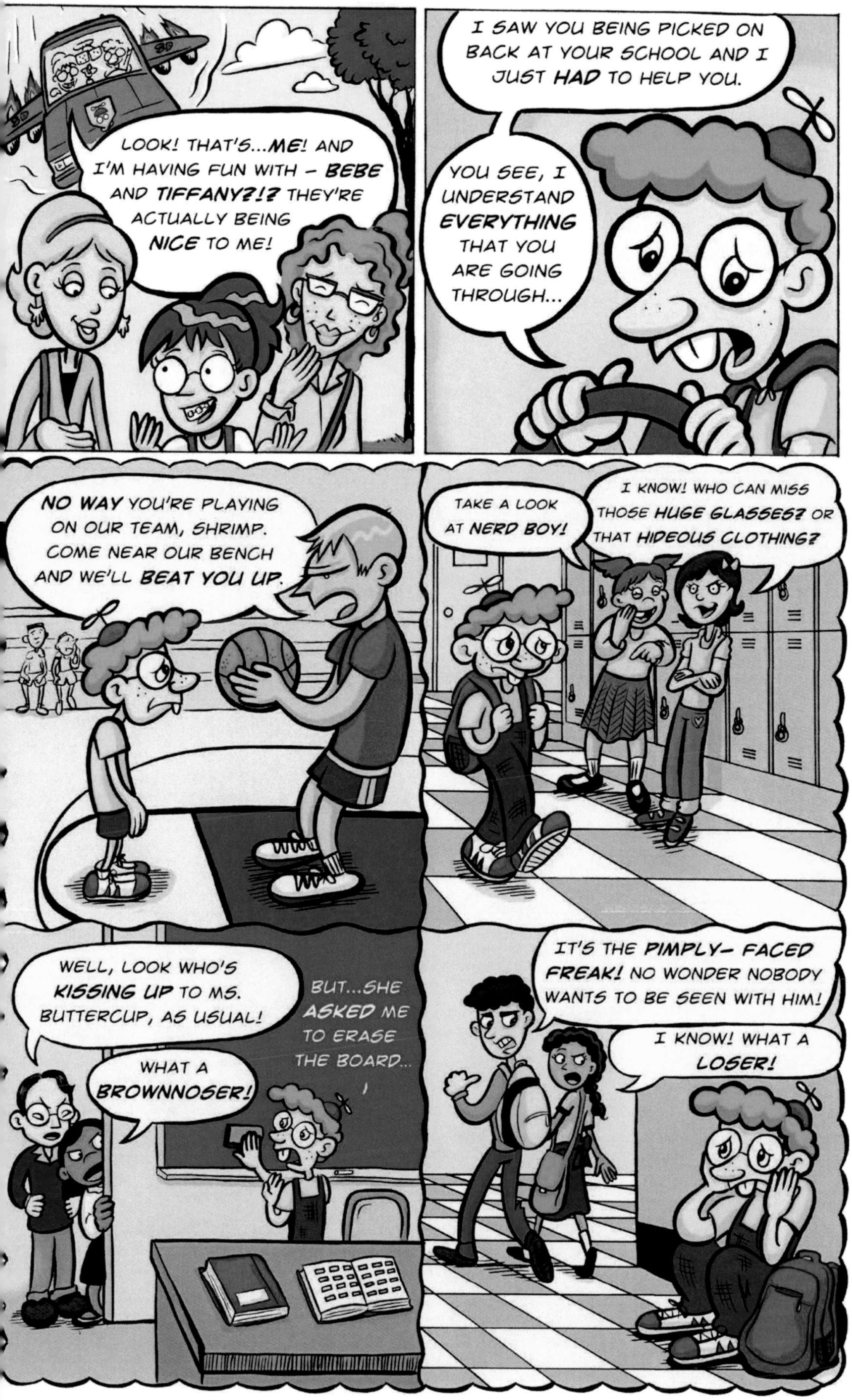
LOOK! THAT'S...ME! AND I'M HAVING FUN WITH – BEBE AND TIFFANY?!? THEY'RE ACTUALLY BEING NICE TO ME!
I SAW YOU BEING PICKED ON BACK AT YOUR SCHOOL AND I JUST HAD TO HELP YOU.
YOU SEE, I UNDERSTAND EVERYTHING THAT YOU ARE GOING THROUGH...
NO WAY YOU'RE PLAYING ON OUR TEAM, SHRIMP. COME NEAR OUR BENCH AND WE'LL BEAT YOU UP.
TAKE A LOOK AT NERD BOY!
I KNOW! WHO CAN MISS THOSE HUGE GLASSES? OR THAT HIDEOUS CLOTHING?
WELL, LOOK WHO'S KISSING UP TO MS. BUTTERCUP, AS USUAL!
WHAT A BROWNNOSER!
BUT...SHE ASKED ME TO ERASE THE BOARD...!
IT'S THE PIMPLY- FACED FREAK! NO WONDER NOBODY WANTS TO BE SEEN WITH HIM!
I KNOW! WHAT A LOSER!

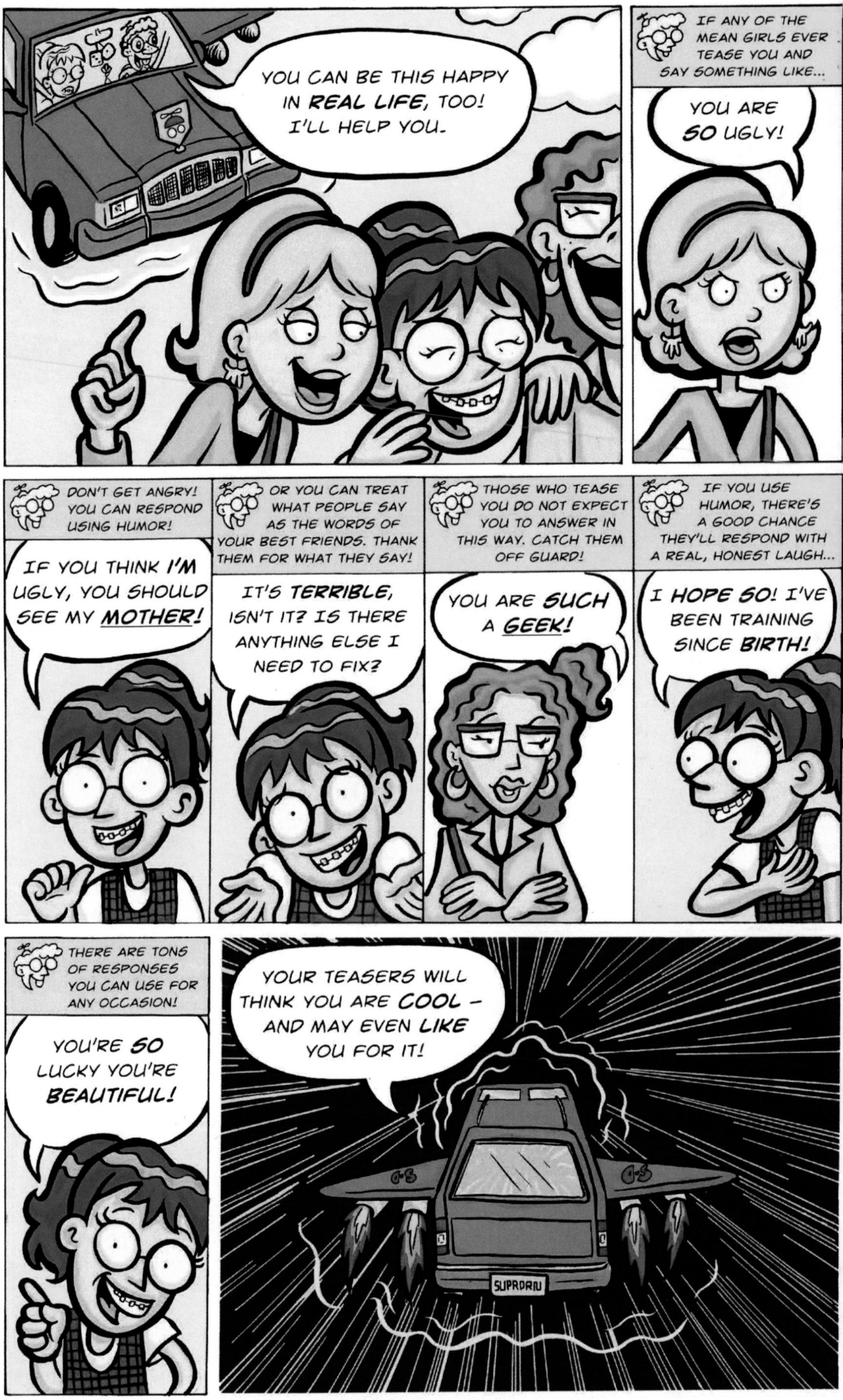
YOU CAN BE THIS HAPPY IN REAL LIFE, TOO! I'LL HELP YOU.
IF ANY OF THE MEAN GIRLS EVER TEASE YOU AND SAY SOMETHING LIKE...
YOU ARE SO UGLY!
DON'T GET ANGRY! YOU CAN RESPOND USING HUMOR!
IF YOU THINK I'M UGLY, YOU SHOULD SEE MY MOTHER!
OR YOU CAN TREAT WHAT PEOPLE SAY AS THE WORDS OF YOUR BEST FRIENDS. THANK THEM FOR WHAT THEY SAY!
IT'S TERRIBLE, ISN'T IT? IS THERE ANYTHING ELSE I NEED TO FIX?
THOSE WHO TEASE YOU DO NOT EXPECT YOU TO ANSWER IN THIS WAY. CATCH THEM OFF GUARD!
YOU ARE SUCH A GEEK!
IF YOU USE HUMOR, THERE'S A GOOD CHANCE THEY'LL RESPOND WITH A REAL, HONEST LAUGH...
I HOPE SO! I'VE BEEN TRAINING SINCE BIRTH!
THERE ARE TONS OF RESPONSES YOU CAN USE FOR ANY OCCASION!
YOU'RE SO LUCKY YOU'RE BEAUTIFUL!
YOUR TEASERS WILL THINK YOU ARE COOL – AND MAY EVEN LIKE YOU FOR IT!
SUPRDAU

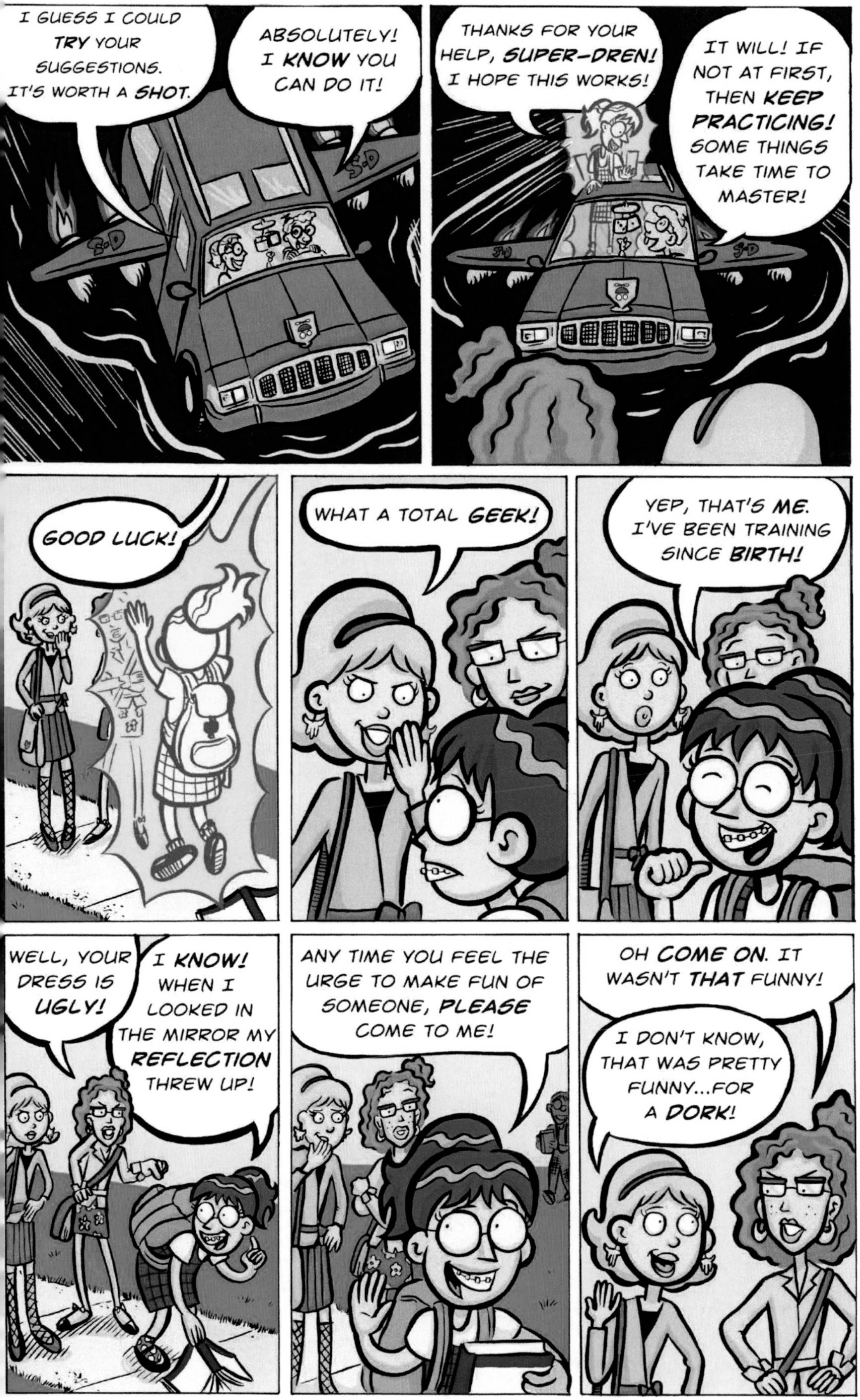
I GUESS I COULD TRY YOUR SUGGESTIONS. IT'S WORTH A SHOT.
ABSOLUTELY! I KNOW YOU CAN DO IT!
THANKS FOR YOUR HELP, SUPER-DREN! I HOPE THIS WORKS!
IT WILL! IF NOT AT FIRST, THEN KEEP PRACTICING! SOME THINGS TAKE TIME TO MASTER!
GOOD LUCK!
WHAT A TOTAL GEEK!
YEP, THAT'S ME. I'VE BEEN TRAINING SINCE BIRTH!
WELL, YOUR DRESS IS UGLY!
I KNOW! WHEN I LOOKED IN THE MIRROR MY REFLECTION THREW UP!
ANY TIME YOU FEEL THE URGE TO MAKE FUN OF SOMEONE, PLEASE COME TO ME!
OH COME ON. IT WASN'T THAT FUNNY!
I DON'T KNOW, THAT WAS PRETTY FUNNY...FOR A DORK!

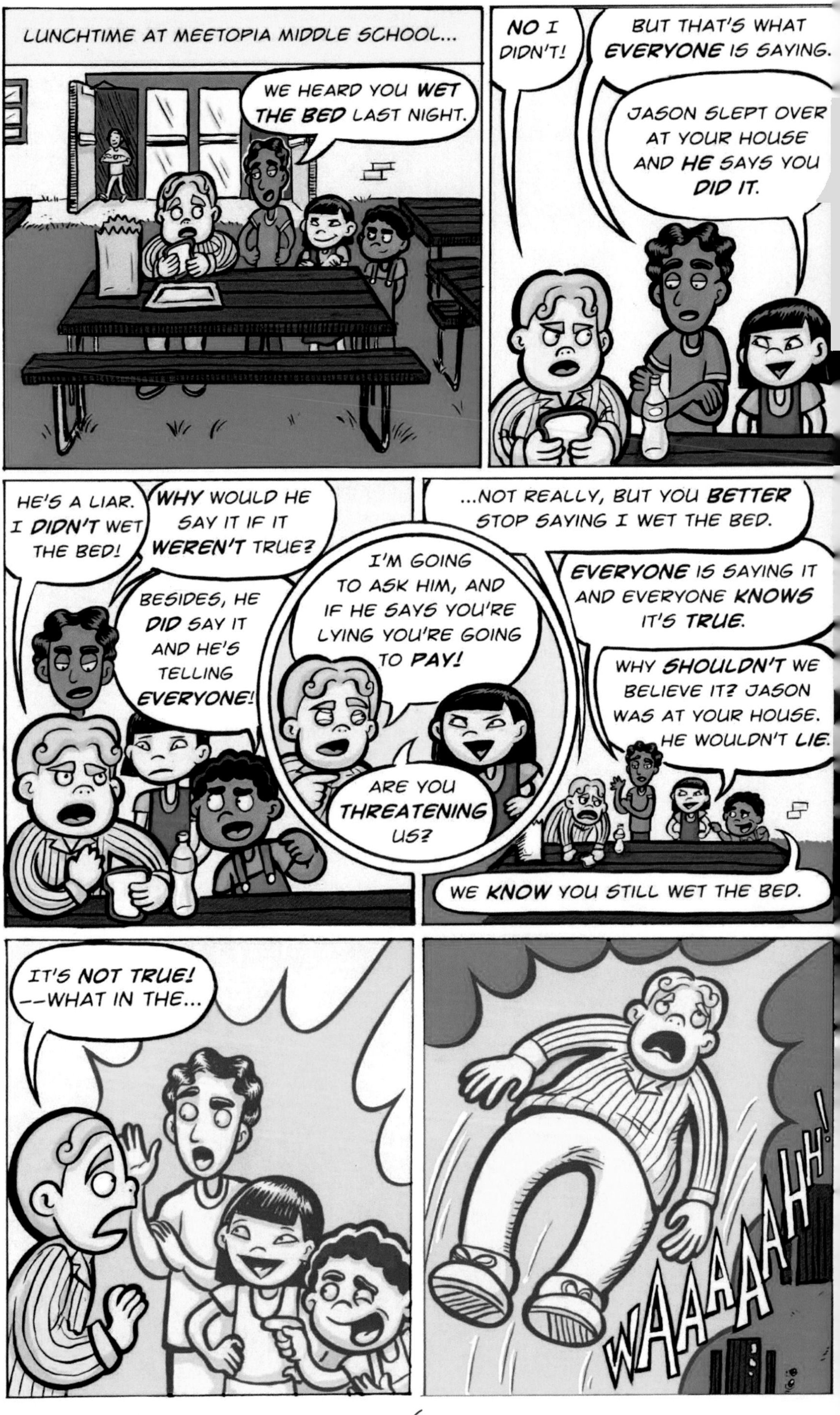
LUNCHTIME AT MEETOPIA MIDDLE SCHOOL...
WE HEARD YOU WET THE BED LAST NIGHT.
NO I DIDN'T!
BUT THAT'S WHAT EVERYONE IS SAYING.
JASON SLEPT OVER AT YOUR HOUSE AND HE SAYS YOU DID IT.
HE'S A LIAR. I DIDN'T WET THE BED!
WHY WOULD HE SAY IT IF IT WEREN'T TRUE?
BESIDES, HE DID SAY IT AND HE'S TELLING EVERYONE!
I'M GOING TO ASK HIM, AND IF HE SAYS YOU'RE LYING YOU'RE GOING TO PAY!
ARE YOU THREATENING US?
...NOT REALLY, BUT YOU BETTER STOP SAYING I WET THE BED.
EVERYONE IS SAYING IT AND EVERYONE KNOWS IT'S TRUE.
WHY SHOULDN'T WE BELIEVE IT? JASON WAS AT YOUR HOUSE. HE WOULDN'T LIE.
WE KNOW YOU STILL WET THE BED.
IT'S NOT TRUE! --WHAT IN THE...
WAAAAAHH!

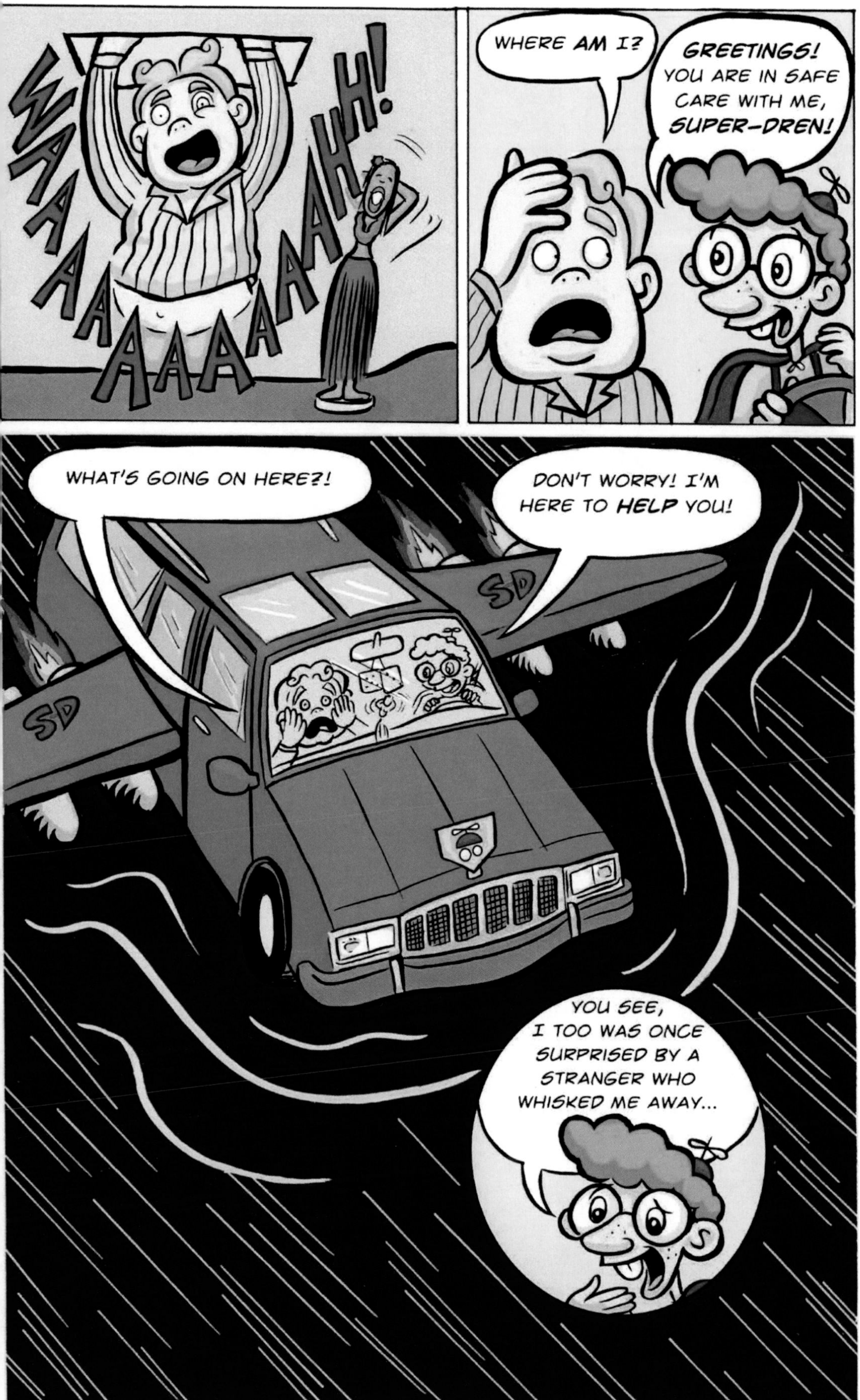
WAAAAAAAAAAAAAH!
WHERE AM I?
GREETINGS! YOU ARE IN SAFE CARE WITH ME, SUPER-DREN!
WHAT'S GOING ON HERE?!
DON'T WORRY! I'M HERE TO HELP YOU!
SD
SD
YOU SEE, I TOO WAS ONCE SURPRISED BY A STRANGER WHO WHISKED ME AWAY...

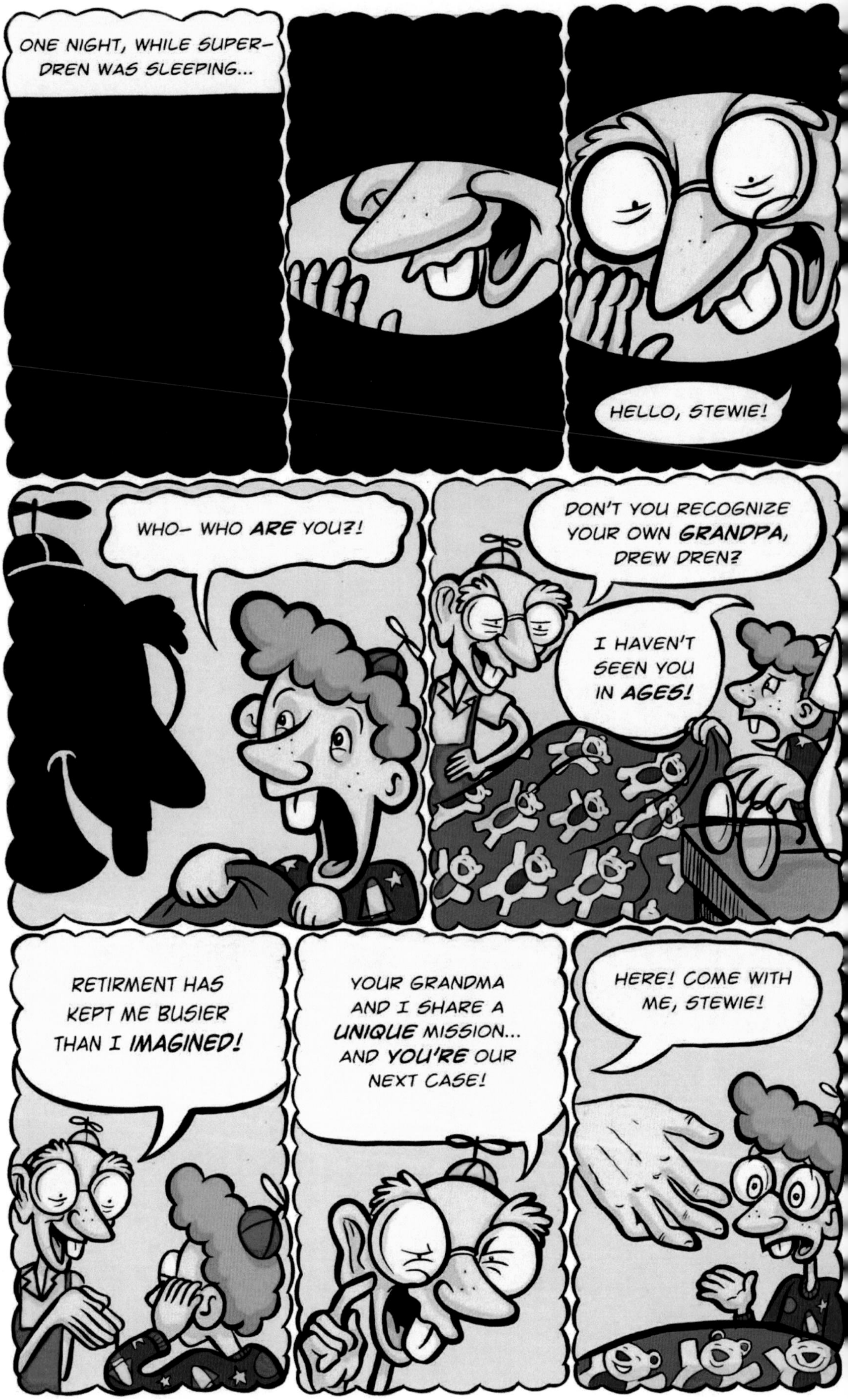
ONE NIGHT, WHILE SUPER-DREN WAS SLEEPING...
HELLO, STEWIE!
WHO- WHO **ARE** YOU?!
DON'T YOU RECOGNIZE YOUR OWN **GRANDPA**, DREW DREN?
I HAVEN'T SEEN YOU IN **AGES!**
RETIRMENT HAS KEPT ME BUSIER THAN I **IMAGINED!**
YOUR GRANDMA AND I SHARE A **UNIQUE** MISSION... AND **YOU'RE** OUR NEXT CASE!
HERE! COME WITH ME, STEWIE!

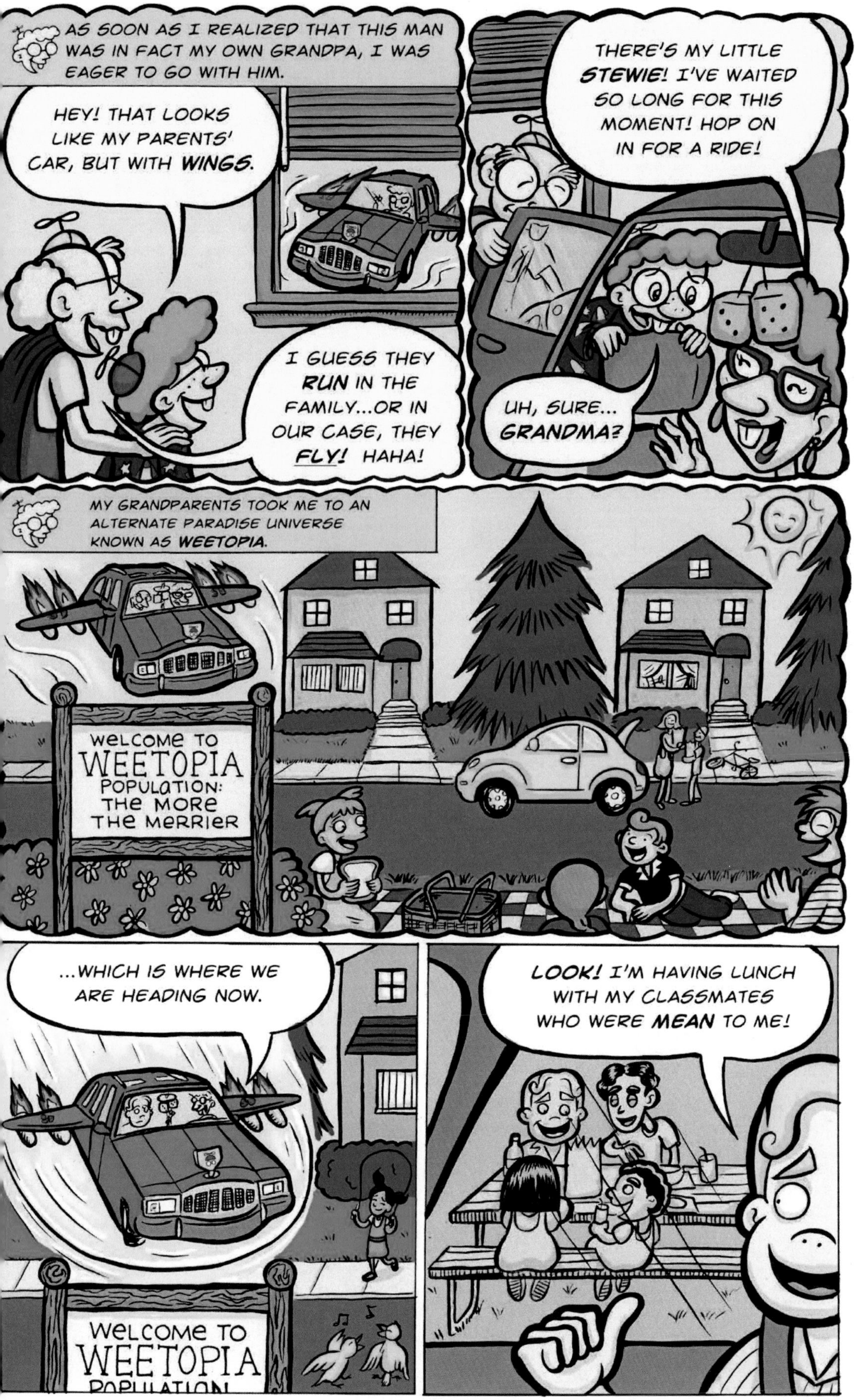
AS SOON AS I REALIZED THAT THIS MAN WAS IN FACT MY OWN GRANDPA, I WAS EAGER TO GO WITH HIM.
HEY! THAT LOOKS LIKE MY PARENTS' CAR, BUT WITH WINGS.
I GUESS THEY RUN IN THE FAMILY...OR IN OUR CASE, THEY FLY! HAHA!
THERE'S MY LITTLE STEWIE! I'VE WAITED SO LONG FOR THIS MOMENT! HOP ON IN FOR A RIDE!
UH, SURE... GRANDMA?
MY GRANDPARENTS TOOK ME TO AN ALTERNATE PARADISE UNIVERSE KNOWN AS WEETOPIA.
WELCOME TO WEETOPIA POPULATION: THE MORE THE MERRIER
...WHICH IS WHERE WE ARE HEADING NOW.
WELCOME TO WEETOPIA
LOOK! I'M HAVING LUNCH WITH MY CLASSMATES WHO WERE MEAN TO ME!

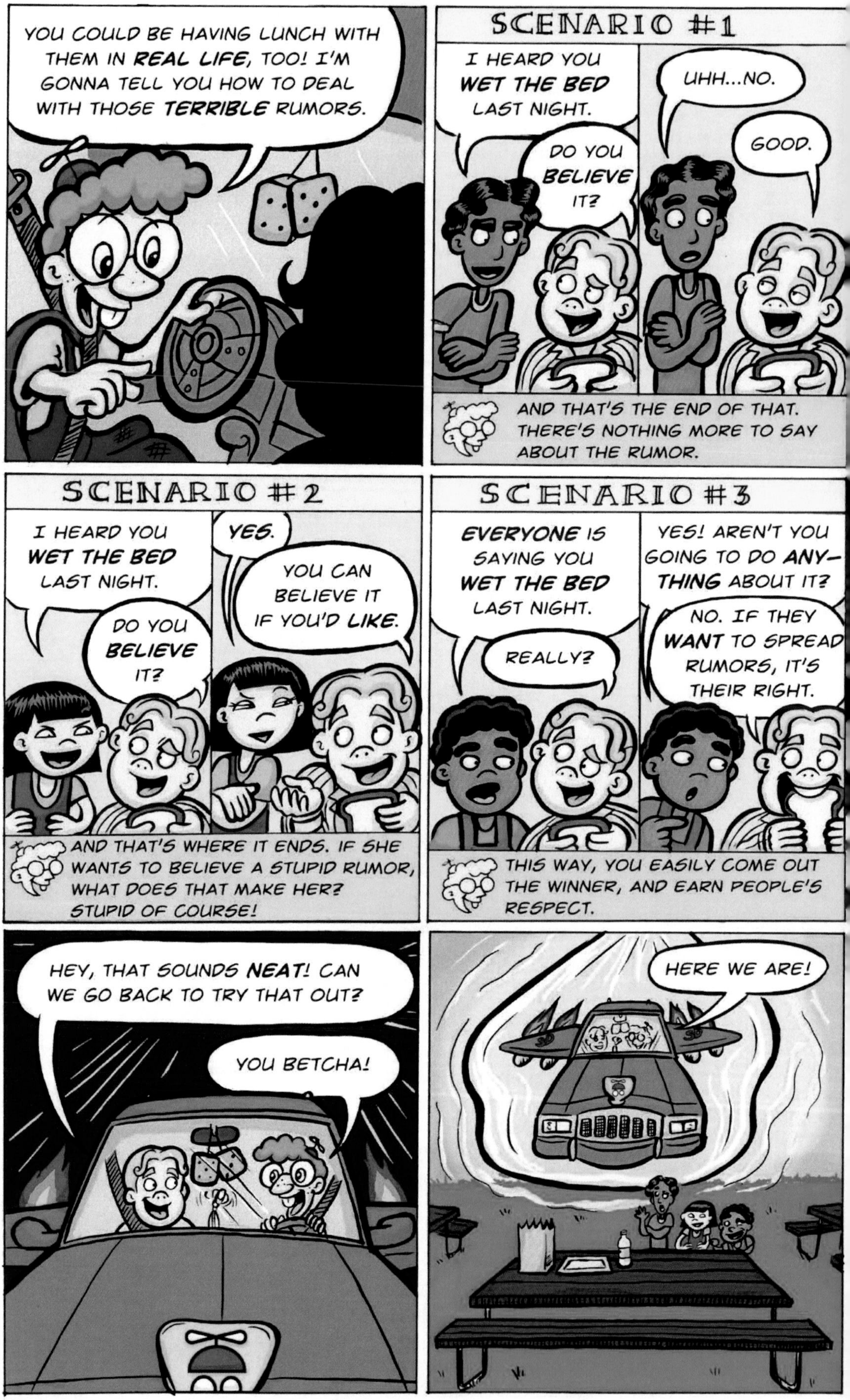

YOU COULD BE HAVING LUNCH WITH THEM IN REAL LIFE, TOO! I'M GONNA TELL YOU HOW TO DEAL WITH THOSE TERRIBLE RUMORS.
SCENARIO #1
I HEARD YOU WET THE BED LAST NIGHT.
DO YOU BELIEVE IT?
UHH...NO.
GOOD.
AND THAT'S THE END OF THAT. THERE'S NOTHING MORE TO SAY ABOUT THE RUMOR.
SCENARIO #2
I HEARD YOU WET THE BED LAST NIGHT.
DO YOU BELIEVE IT?
YES.
YOU CAN BELIEVE IT IF YOU'D LIKE.
AND THAT'S WHERE IT ENDS. IF SHE WANTS TO BELIEVE A STUPID RUMOR, WHAT DOES THAT MAKE HER? STUPID OF COURSE!
SCENARIO #3
EVERYONE IS SAYING YOU WET THE BED LAST NIGHT.
REALLY?
YES! AREN'T YOU GOING TO DO ANY-THING ABOUT IT?
NO. IF THEY WANT TO SPREAD RUMORS, IT'S THEIR RIGHT.
THIS WAY, YOU EASILY COME OUT THE WINNER, AND EARN PEOPLE'S RESPECT.
HEY, THAT SOUNDS NEAT! CAN WE GO BACK TO TRY THAT OUT?
YOU BETCHA!
HERE WE ARE!

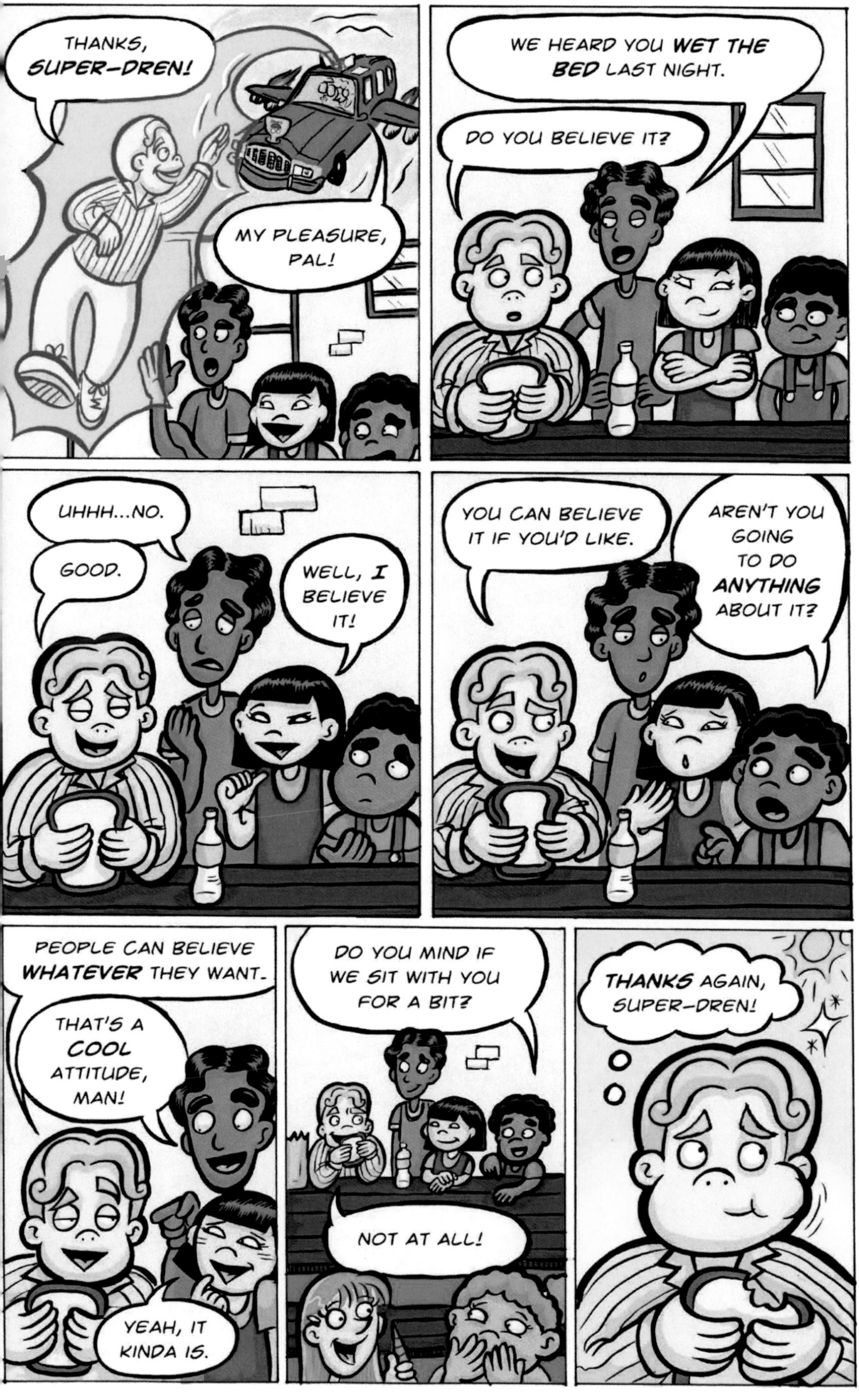
THANKS, SUPER-DREN!
MY PLEASURE, PAL!
WE HEARD YOU WET THE BED LAST NIGHT.
DO YOU BELIEVE IT?
UHHH...NO.
GOOD.
WELL, I BELIEVE IT!
YOU CAN BELIEVE IT IF YOU'D LIKE.
AREN'T YOU GOING TO DO ANYTHING ABOUT IT?
PEOPLE CAN BELIEVE WHATEVER THEY WANT.
THAT'S A COOL ATTITUDE, MAN!
YEAH, IT KINDA IS.
DO YOU MIND IF WE SIT WITH YOU FOR A BIT?
NOT AT ALL!
THANKS AGAIN, SUPER-DREN!

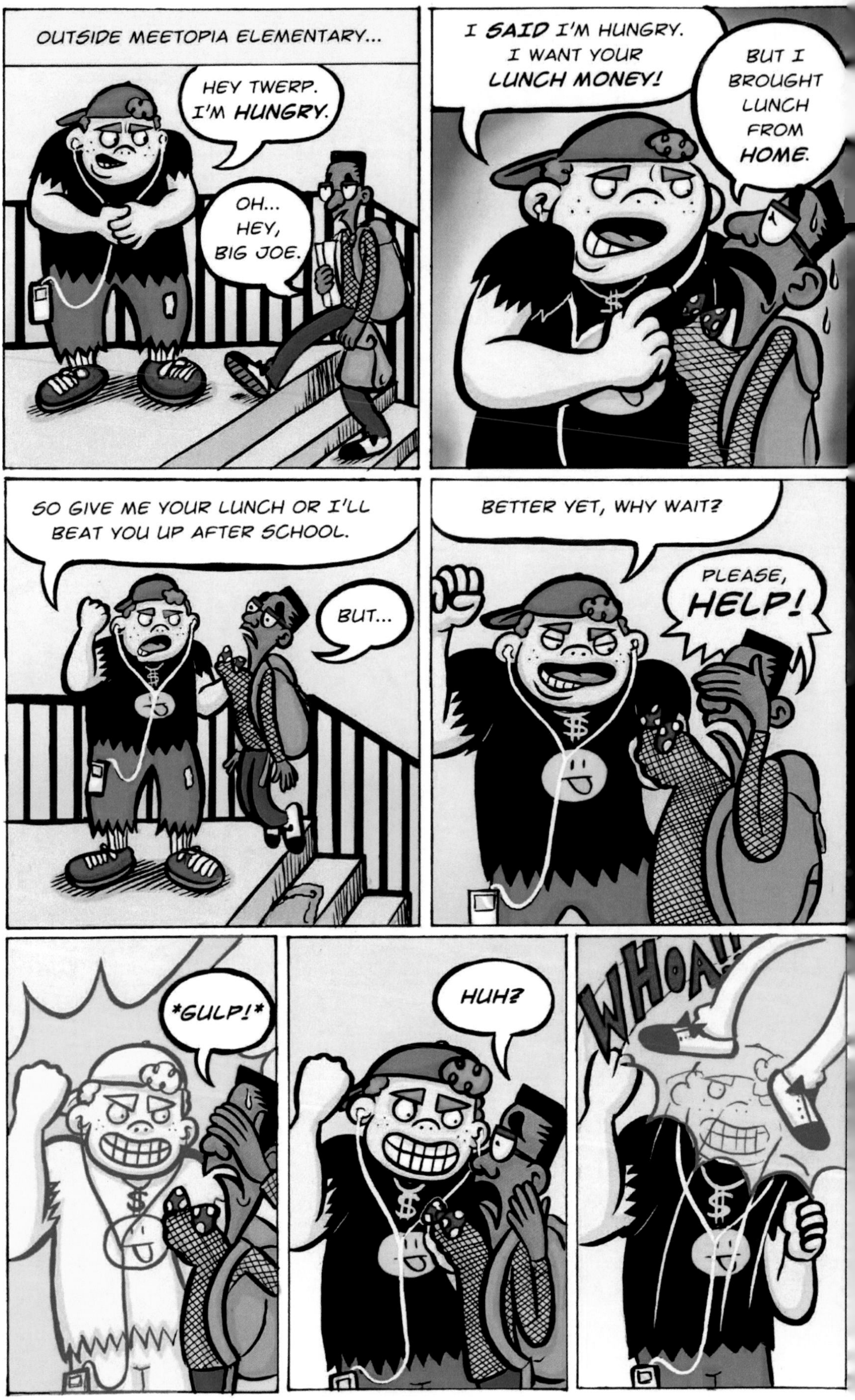
OUTSIDE MEETOPIA ELEMENTARY...
HEY TWERP. I'M HUNGRY.
OH... HEY, BIG JOE.
I SAID I'M HUNGRY. I WANT YOUR LUNCH MONEY!
BUT I BROUGHT LUNCH FROM HOME.
SO GIVE ME YOUR LUNCH OR I'LL BEAT YOU UP AFTER SCHOOL.
BUT...
BETTER YET, WHY WAIT?
PLEASE, HELP!
GULP!
HUH?
WHOA!!

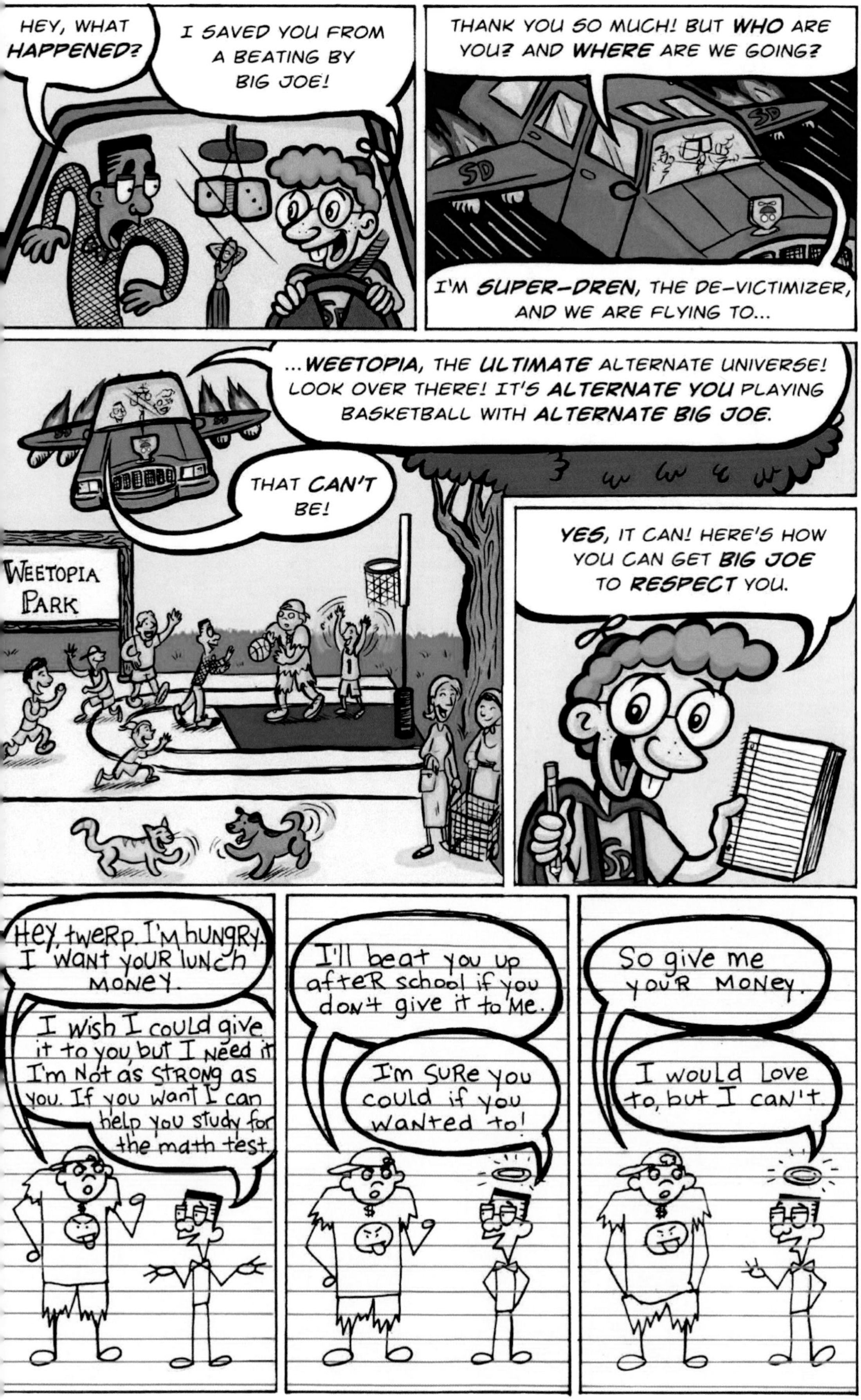
HEY, WHAT HAPPENED?
I SAVED YOU FROM A BEATING BY BIG JOE!
THANK YOU SO MUCH! BUT WHO ARE YOU? AND WHERE ARE WE GOING?
I'M SUPER-DREN, THE DE-VICTIMIZER, AND WE ARE FLYING TO...
...WEETOPIA, THE ULTIMATE ALTERNATE UNIVERSE! LOOK OVER THERE! IT'S ALTERNATE YOU PLAYING BASKETBALL WITH ALTERNATE BIG JOE.
THAT CAN'T BE!
WEETOPIA PARK
YES, IT CAN! HERE'S HOW YOU CAN GET BIG JOE TO RESPECT YOU.
Hey, twerp. I'm hungry. I want your lunch money.
I wish I could give it to you but I need it. I'm not as strong as you. If you want I can help you study for the math test.
I'll beat you up after school if you don't give it to me.
I'm sure you could if you wanted to!
So give me your money.
I would love to, but I can't.

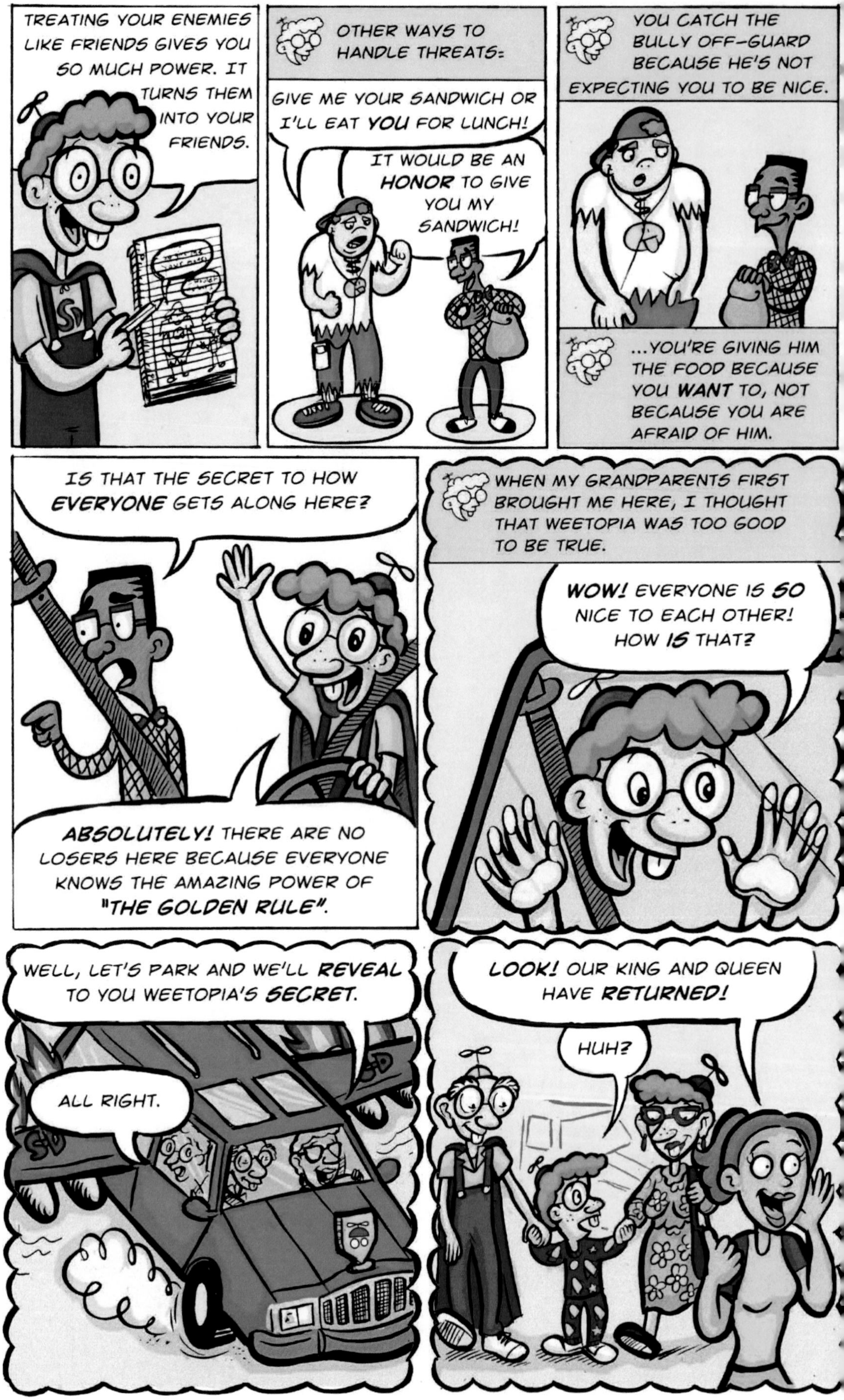

TREATING YOUR ENEMIES LIKE FRIENDS GIVES YOU SO MUCH POWER. IT TURNS THEM INTO YOUR FRIENDS.
OTHER WAYS TO HANDLE THREATS:
GIVE ME YOUR SANDWICH OR I'LL EAT YOU FOR LUNCH!
IT WOULD BE AN HONOR TO GIVE YOU MY SANDWICH!
YOU CATCH THE BULLY OFF-GUARD BECAUSE HE'S NOT EXPECTING YOU TO BE NICE.
...YOU'RE GIVING HIM THE FOOD BECAUSE YOU WANT TO, NOT BECAUSE YOU ARE AFRAID OF HIM.
IS THAT THE SECRET TO HOW EVERYONE GETS ALONG HERE?
ABSOLUTELY! THERE ARE NO LOSERS HERE BECAUSE EVERYONE KNOWS THE AMAZING POWER OF "THE GOLDEN RULE".
WHEN MY GRANDPARENTS FIRST BROUGHT ME HERE, I THOUGHT THAT WEETOPIA WAS TOO GOOD TO BE TRUE.
WOW! EVERYONE IS SO NICE TO EACH OTHER! HOW IS THAT?
WELL, LET'S PARK AND WE'LL REVEAL TO YOU WEETOPIA'S SECRET.
ALL RIGHT.
LOOK! OUR KING AND QUEEN HAVE RETURNED!
HUH?

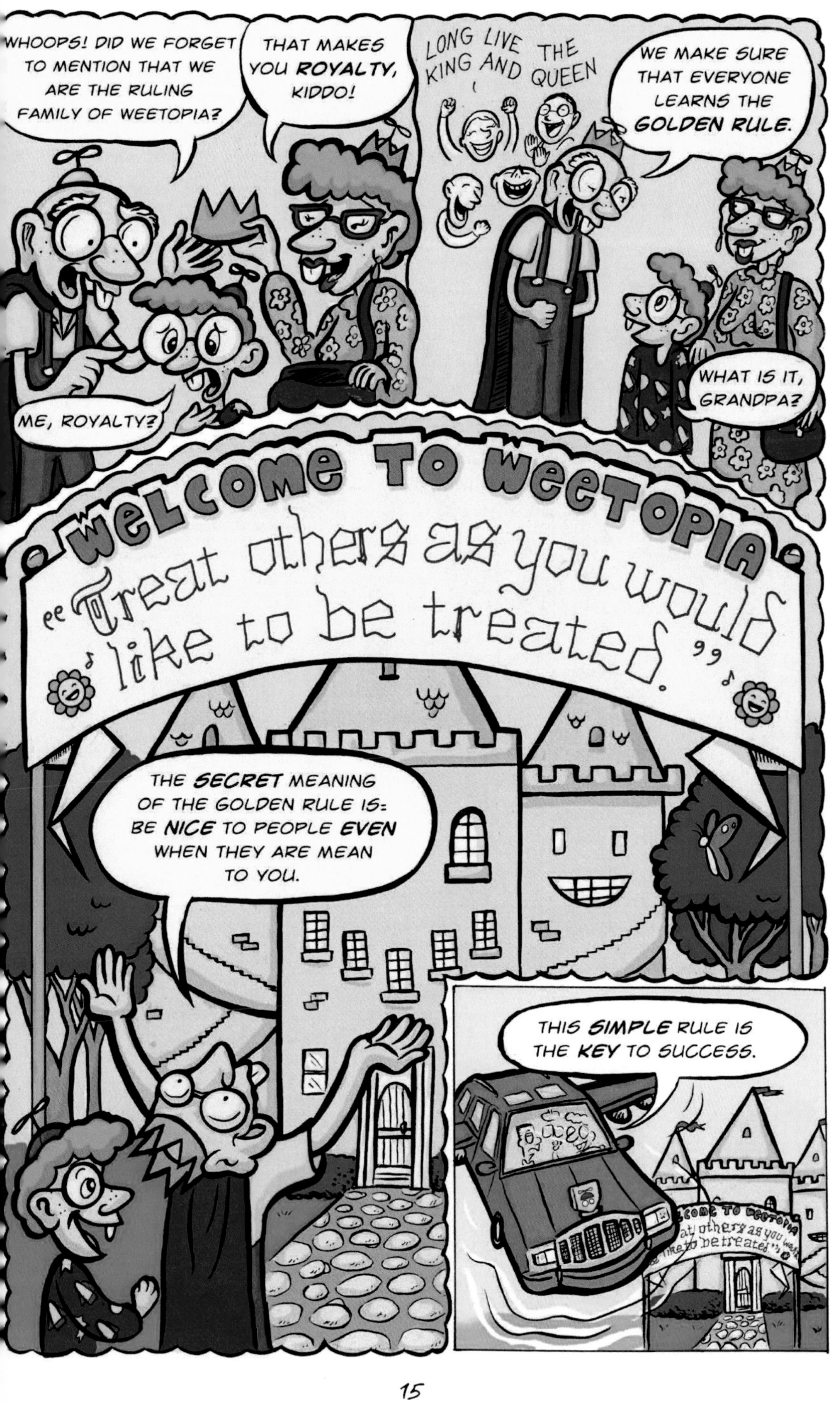
WHOOPS! DID WE FORGET TO MENTION THAT WE ARE THE RULING FAMILY OF WEETOPIA?
THAT MAKES YOU ROYALTY, KIDDO!
ME, ROYALTY?
LONG LIVE THE KING AND QUEEN
WE MAKE SURE THAT EVERYONE LEARNS THE GOLDEN RULE.
WHAT IS IT, GRANDPA?
WELCOME TO WEETOPIA
"Treat others as you would like to be treated."
THE SECRET MEANING OF THE GOLDEN RULE IS: BE NICE TO PEOPLE EVEN WHEN THEY ARE MEAN TO YOU.
THIS SIMPLE RULE IS THE KEY TO SUCCESS.

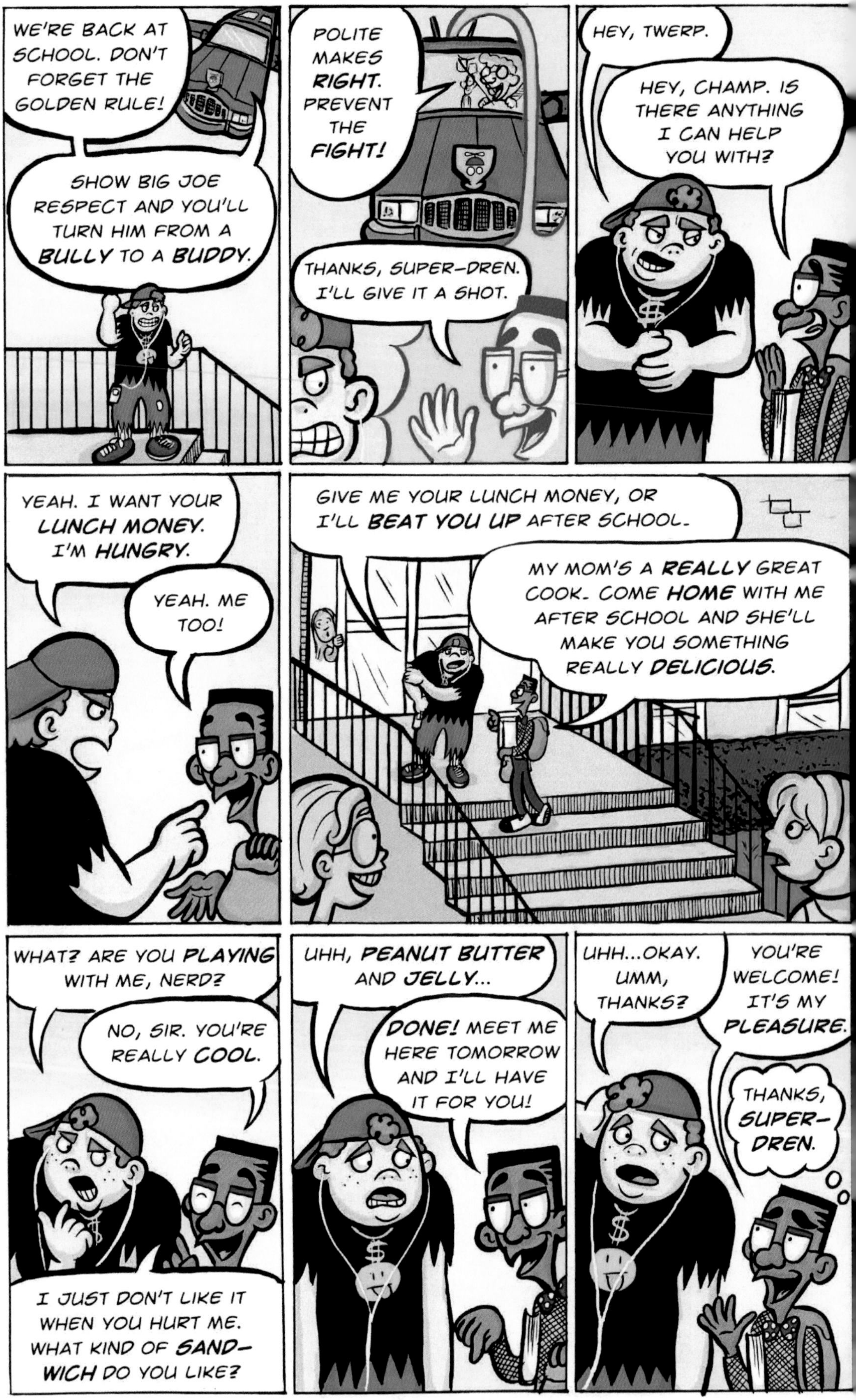
WE'RE BACK AT SCHOOL. DON'T FORGET THE GOLDEN RULE!
SHOW BIG JOE RESPECT AND YOU'LL TURN HIM FROM A BULLY TO A BUDDY.
POLITE MAKES RIGHT. PREVENT THE FIGHT!
THANKS, SUPER-DREN. I'LL GIVE IT A SHOT.
HEY, TWERP.
HEY, CHAMP. IS THERE ANYTHING I CAN HELP YOU WITH?
YEAH. I WANT YOUR LUNCH MONEY. I'M HUNGRY.
YEAH. ME TOO!
GIVE ME YOUR LUNCH MONEY, OR I'LL BEAT YOU UP AFTER SCHOOL.
MY MOM'S A REALLY GREAT COOK. COME HOME WITH ME AFTER SCHOOL AND SHE'LL MAKE YOU SOMETHING REALLY DELICIOUS.
WHAT? ARE YOU PLAYING WITH ME, NERD?
NO, SIR. YOU'RE REALLY COOL.
I JUST DON'T LIKE IT WHEN YOU HURT ME. WHAT KIND OF SAND-WICH DO YOU LIKE?
UHH, PEANUT BUTTER AND JELLY...
DONE! MEET ME HERE TOMORROW AND I'LL HAVE IT FOR YOU!
UHH...OKAY. UMM, THANKS?
YOU'RE WELCOME! IT'S MY PLEASURE.
THANKS, SUPER-DREN.

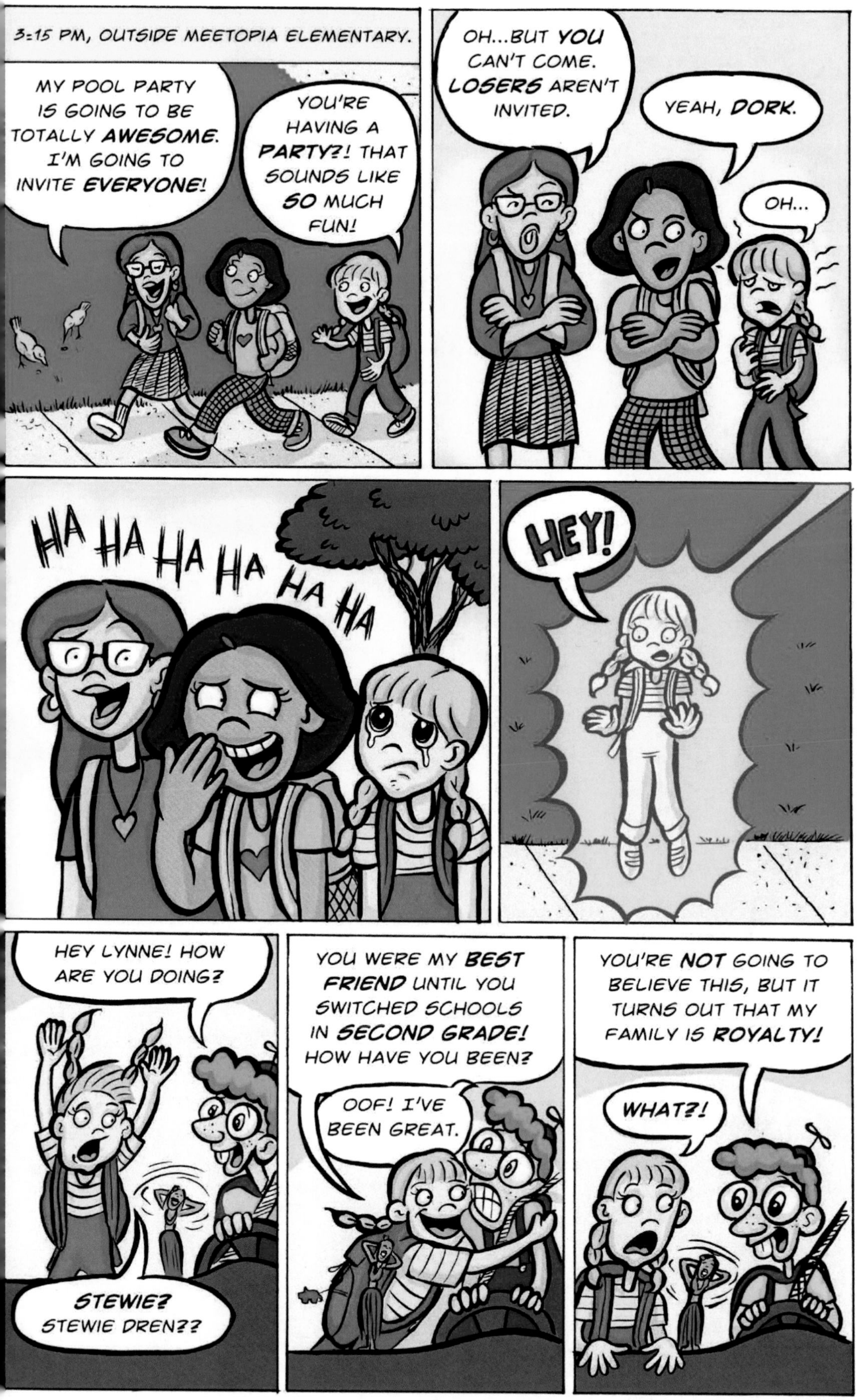
3:15 PM, OUTSIDE MEETOPIA ELEMENTARY.
MY POOL PARTY IS GOING TO BE TOTALLY AWESOME. I'M GOING TO INVITE EVERYONE!
YOU'RE HAVING A PARTY?! THAT SOUNDS LIKE SO MUCH FUN!
OH...BUT YOU CAN'T COME. LOSERS AREN'T INVITED.
YEAH, DORK.
OH...
HA HA HA HA HA HA
HEY!
HEY LYNNE! HOW ARE YOU DOING?
STEWIE? STEWIE DREN??
YOU WERE MY BEST FRIEND UNTIL YOU SWITCHED SCHOOLS IN SECOND GRADE! HOW HAVE YOU BEEN?
OOF! I'VE BEEN GREAT.
YOU'RE NOT GOING TO BELIEVE THIS, BUT IT TURNS OUT THAT MY FAMILY IS ROYALTY!
WHAT?!

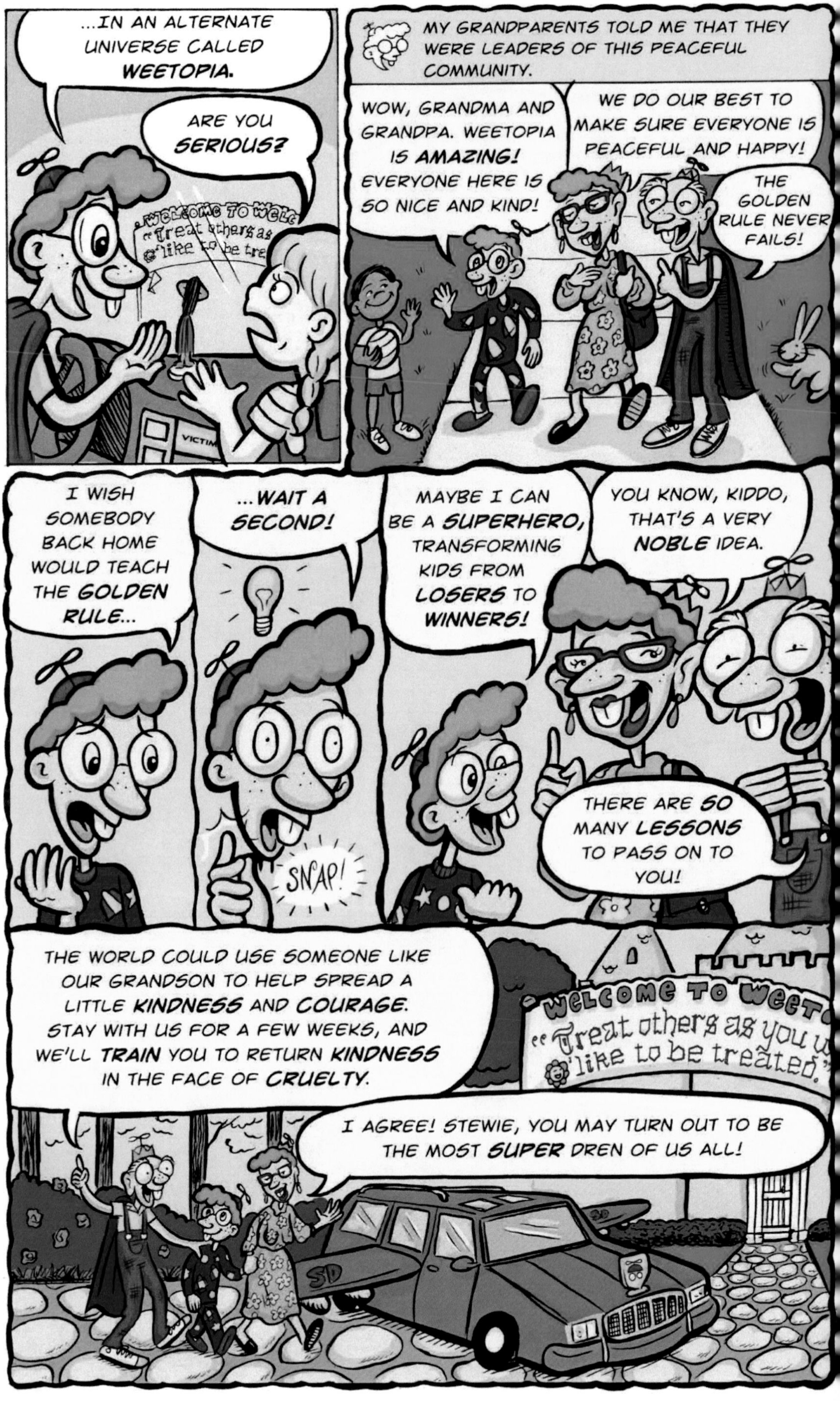
...IN AN ALTERNATE UNIVERSE CALLED WEETOPIA.
ARE YOU SERIOUS?
MY GRANDPARENTS TOLD ME THAT THEY WERE LEADERS OF THIS PEACEFUL COMMUNITY.
WOW, GRANDMA AND GRANDPA. WEETOPIA IS AMAZING! EVERYONE HERE IS SO NICE AND KIND!
WE DO OUR BEST TO MAKE SURE EVERYONE IS PEACEFUL AND HAPPY!
THE GOLDEN RULE NEVER FAILS!
I WISH SOMEBODY BACK HOME WOULD TEACH THE GOLDEN RULE...
...WAIT A SECOND!
SNAP!
MAYBE I CAN BE A SUPERHERO, TRANSFORMING KIDS FROM LOSERS TO WINNERS!
YOU KNOW, KIDDO, THAT'S A VERY NOBLE IDEA.
THERE ARE SO MANY LESSONS TO PASS ON TO YOU!
THE WORLD COULD USE SOMEONE LIKE OUR GRANDSON TO HELP SPREAD A LITTLE KINDNESS AND COURAGE. STAY WITH US FOR A FEW WEEKS, AND WE'LL TRAIN YOU TO RETURN KINDNESS IN THE FACE OF CRUELTY.
WELCOME TO WEET
"Treat others as you w
like to be treated."
I AGREE! STEWIE, YOU MAY TURN OUT TO BE THE MOST SUPER DREN OF US ALL!

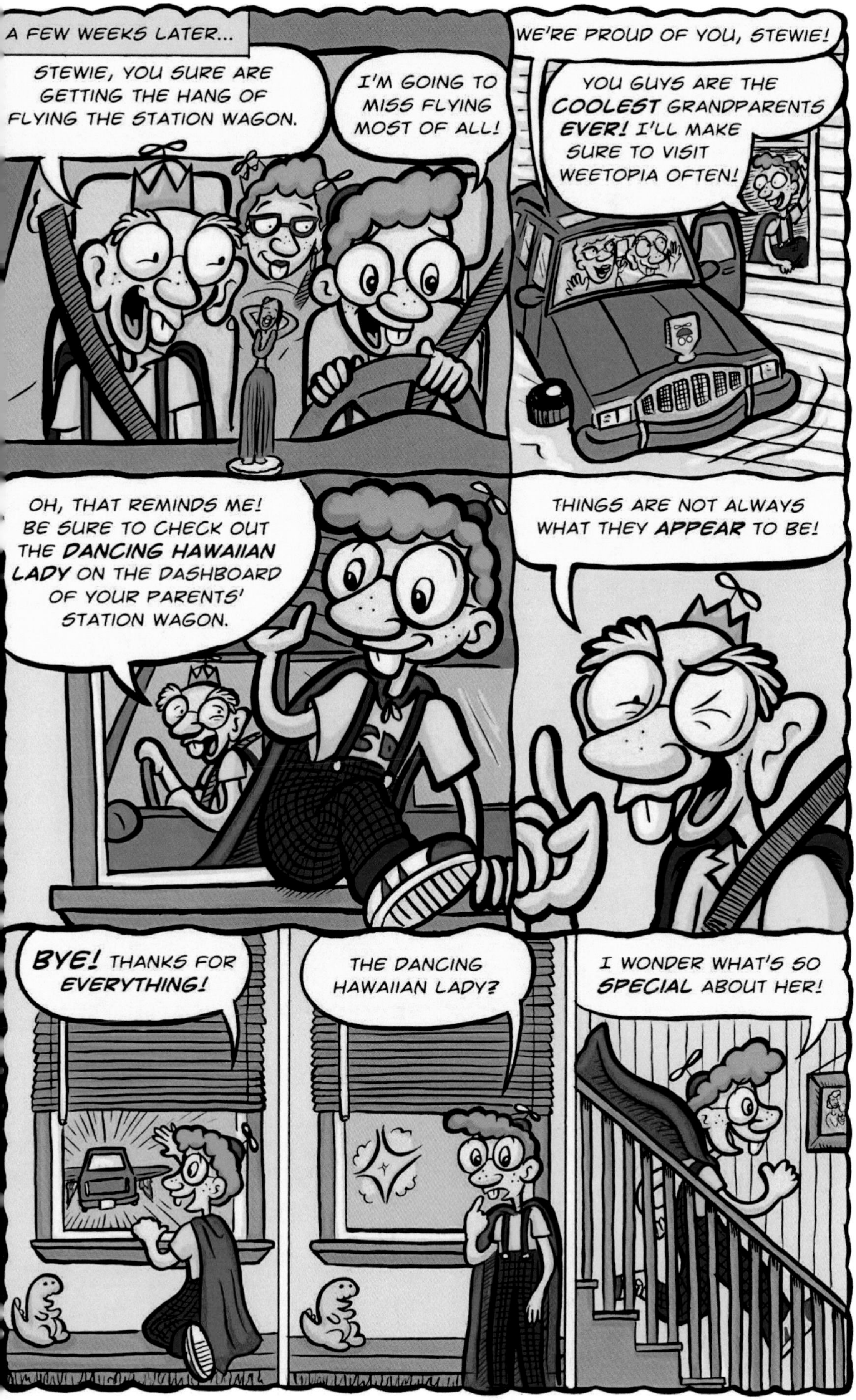
A FEW WEEKS LATER...
STEWIE, YOU SURE ARE GETTING THE HANG OF FLYING THE STATION WAGON.
I'M GOING TO MISS FLYING MOST OF ALL!
WE'RE PROUD OF YOU, STEWIE!
YOU GUYS ARE THE COOLEST GRANDPARENTS EVER! I'LL MAKE SURE TO VISIT WEETOPIA OFTEN!
OH, THAT REMINDS ME! BE SURE TO CHECK OUT THE DANCING HAWAIIAN LADY ON THE DASHBOARD OF YOUR PARENTS' STATION WAGON.
THINGS ARE NOT ALWAYS WHAT THEY APPEAR TO BE!
BYE! THANKS FOR EVERYTHING!
THE DANCING HAWAIIAN LADY?
I WONDER WHAT'S SO SPECIAL ABOUT HER!

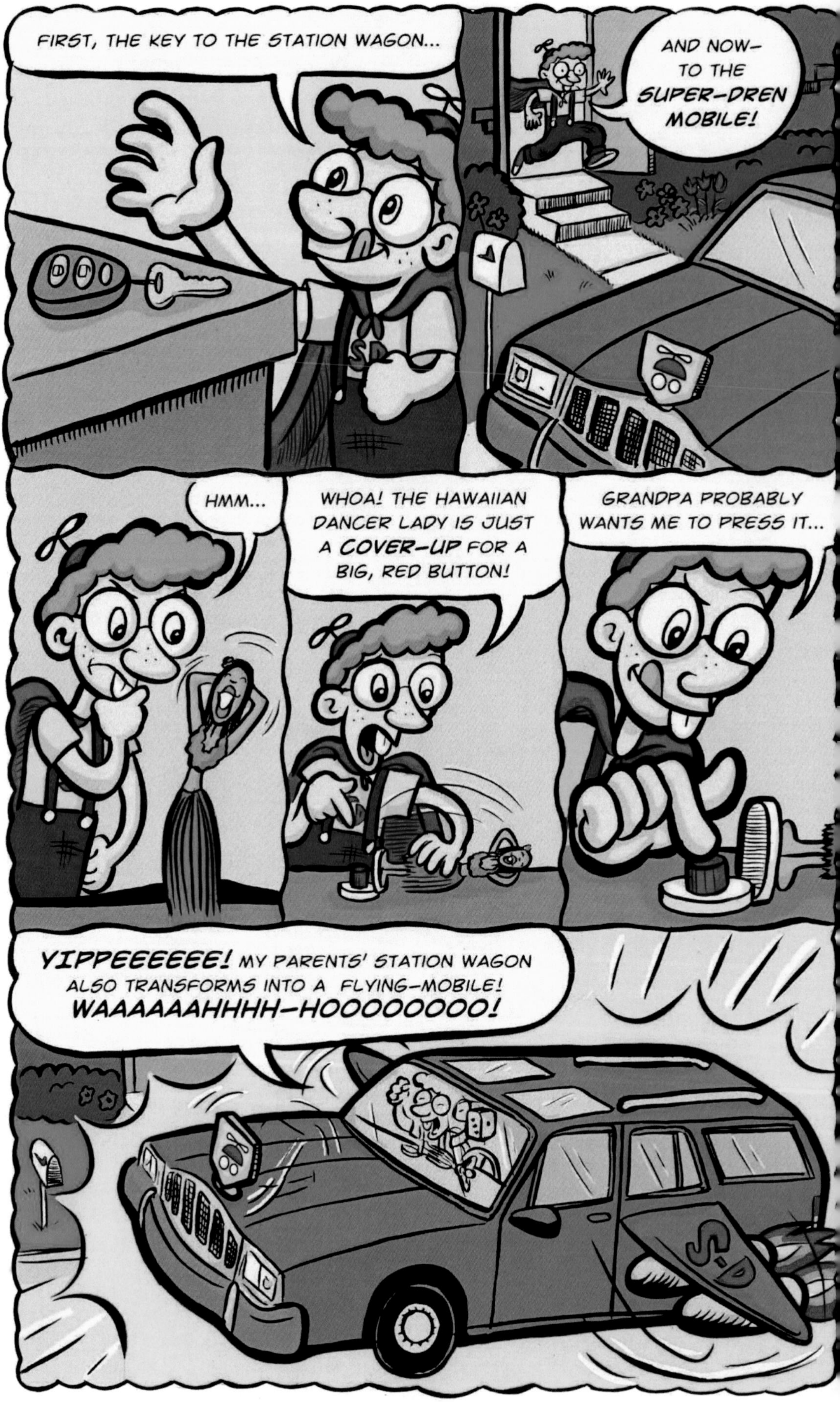
FIRST, THE KEY TO THE STATION WAGON...
AND NOW— TO THE SUPER-DREN MOBILE!
HMM...
WHOA! THE HAWAIIAN DANCER LADY IS JUST A COVER-UP FOR A BIG, RED BUTTON!
GRANDPA PROBABLY WANTS ME TO PRESS IT...
YIPPEEEEEEE! MY PARENTS' STATION WAGON ALSO TRANSFORMS INTO A FLYING-MOBILE!
WAAAAAAHHHH-HOOOOOOOO!

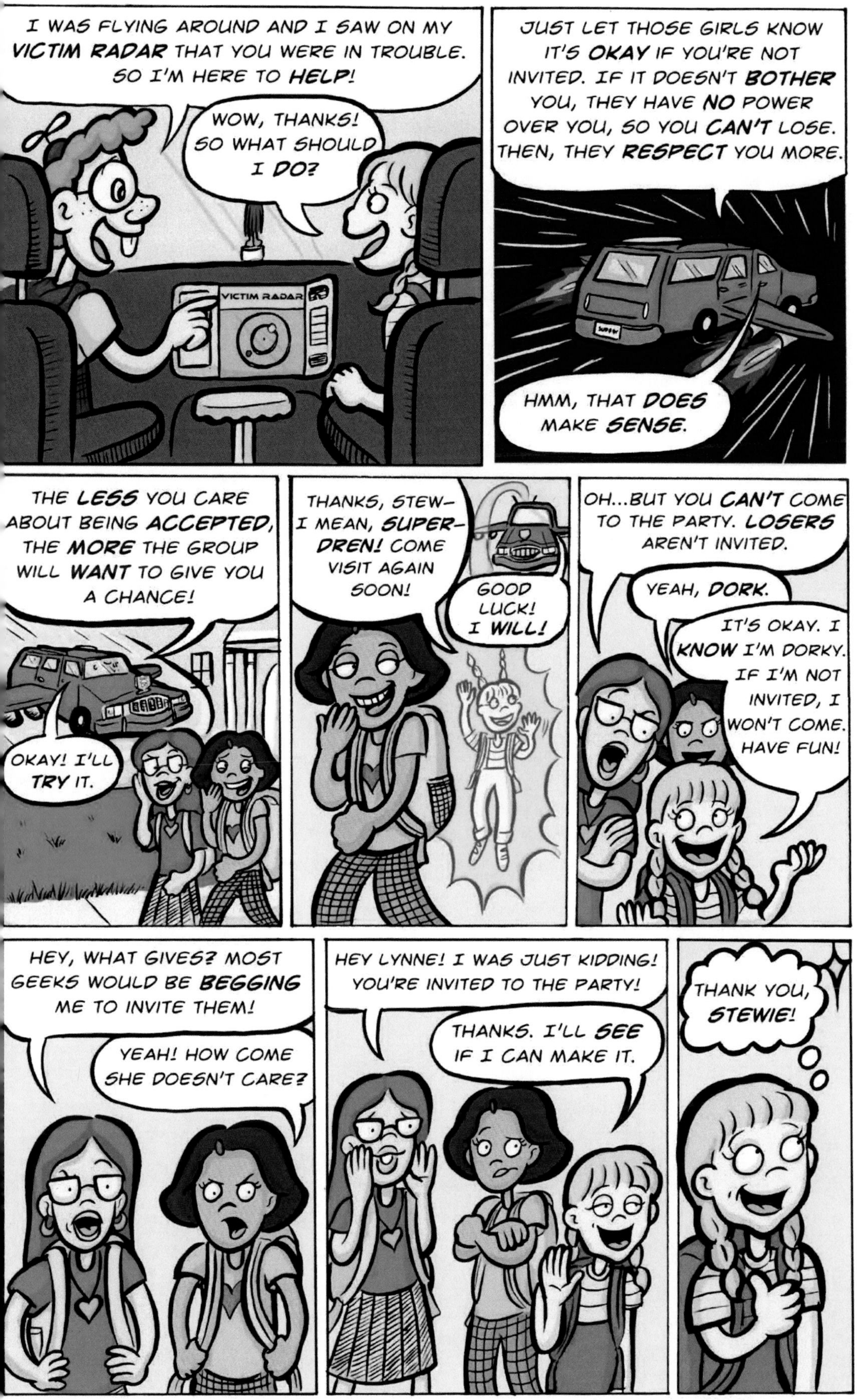
I WAS FLYING AROUND AND I SAW ON MY VICTIM RADAR THAT YOU WERE IN TROUBLE. SO I'M HERE TO HELP!
WOW, THANKS! SO WHAT SHOULD I DO?
VICTIM RADAR
JUST LET THOSE GIRLS KNOW IT'S OKAY IF YOU'RE NOT INVITED. IF IT DOESN'T BOTHER YOU, THEY HAVE NO POWER OVER YOU, SO YOU CAN'T LOSE. THEN, THEY RESPECT YOU MORE.
HMM, THAT DOES MAKE SENSE.
THE LESS YOU CARE ABOUT BEING ACCEPTED, THE MORE THE GROUP WILL WANT TO GIVE YOU A CHANCE!
OKAY! I'LL TRY IT.
THANKS, STEW– I MEAN, SUPER-DREN! COME VISIT AGAIN SOON!
GOOD LUCK!
I WILL!
OH...BUT YOU CAN'T COME TO THE PARTY. LOSERS AREN'T INVITED.
YEAH, DORK.
IT'S OKAY. I KNOW I'M DORKY. IF I'M NOT INVITED, I WON'T COME. HAVE FUN!
HEY, WHAT GIVES? MOST GEEKS WOULD BE BEGGING ME TO INVITE THEM!
YEAH! HOW COME SHE DOESN'T CARE?
HEY LYNNE! I WAS JUST KIDDING! YOU'RE INVITED TO THE PARTY!
THANKS. I'LL SEE IF I CAN MAKE IT.
THANK YOU, STEWIE!

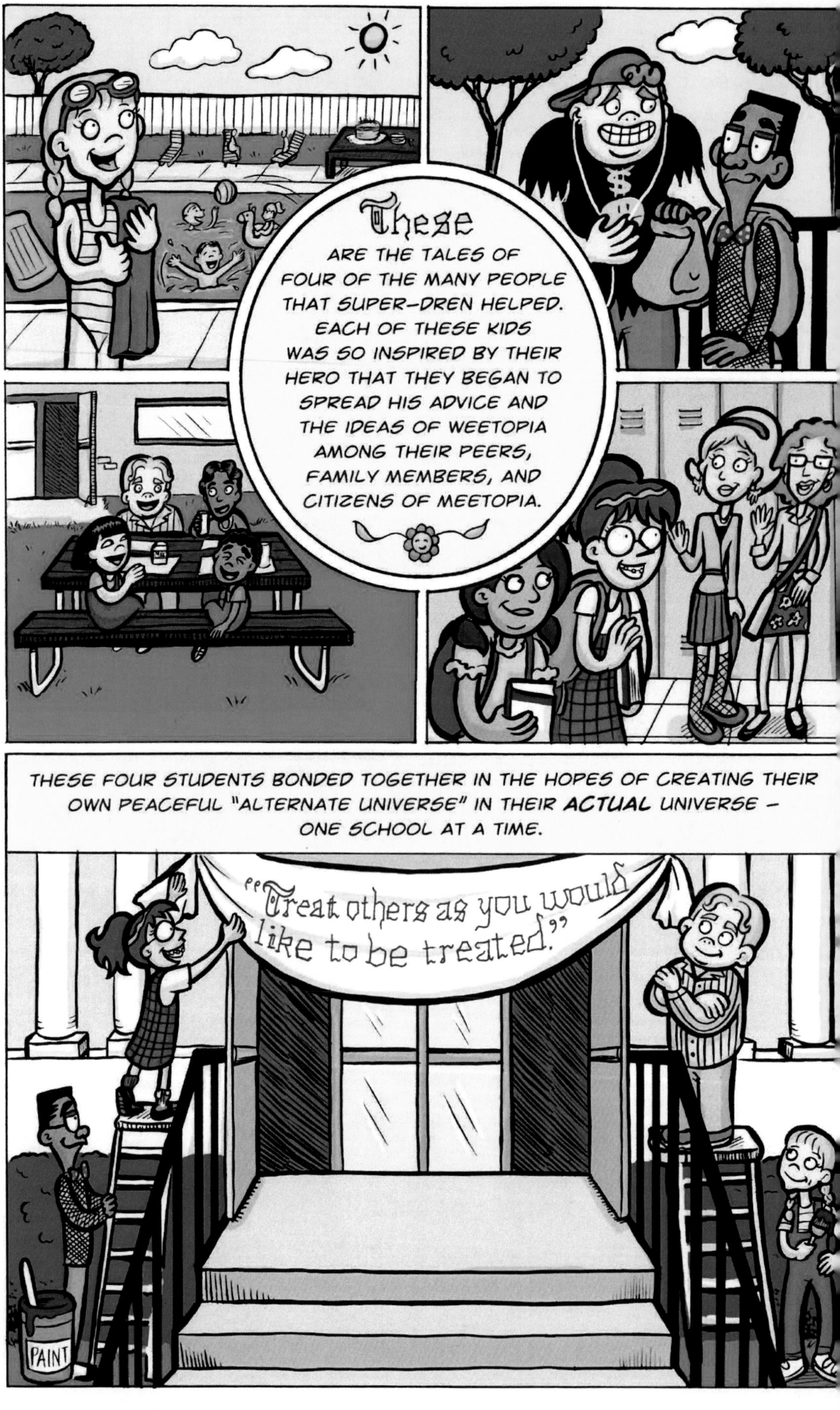
These
ARE THE TALES OF FOUR OF THE MANY PEOPLE THAT SUPER-DREN HELPED. EACH OF THESE KIDS WAS SO INSPIRED BY THEIR HERO THAT THEY BEGAN TO SPREAD HIS ADVICE AND THE IDEAS OF WEETOPIA AMONG THEIR PEERS, FAMILY MEMBERS, AND CITIZENS OF MEETOPIA.
THESE FOUR STUDENTS BONDED TOGETHER IN THE HOPES OF CREATING THEIR OWN PEACEFUL "ALTERNATE UNIVERSE" IN THEIR ACTUAL UNIVERSE – ONE SCHOOL AT A TIME.
"Treat others as you would like to be treated."
PAINT

A MESSAGE FROM
SUPER-DREN
(BY IZZY KALMAN)

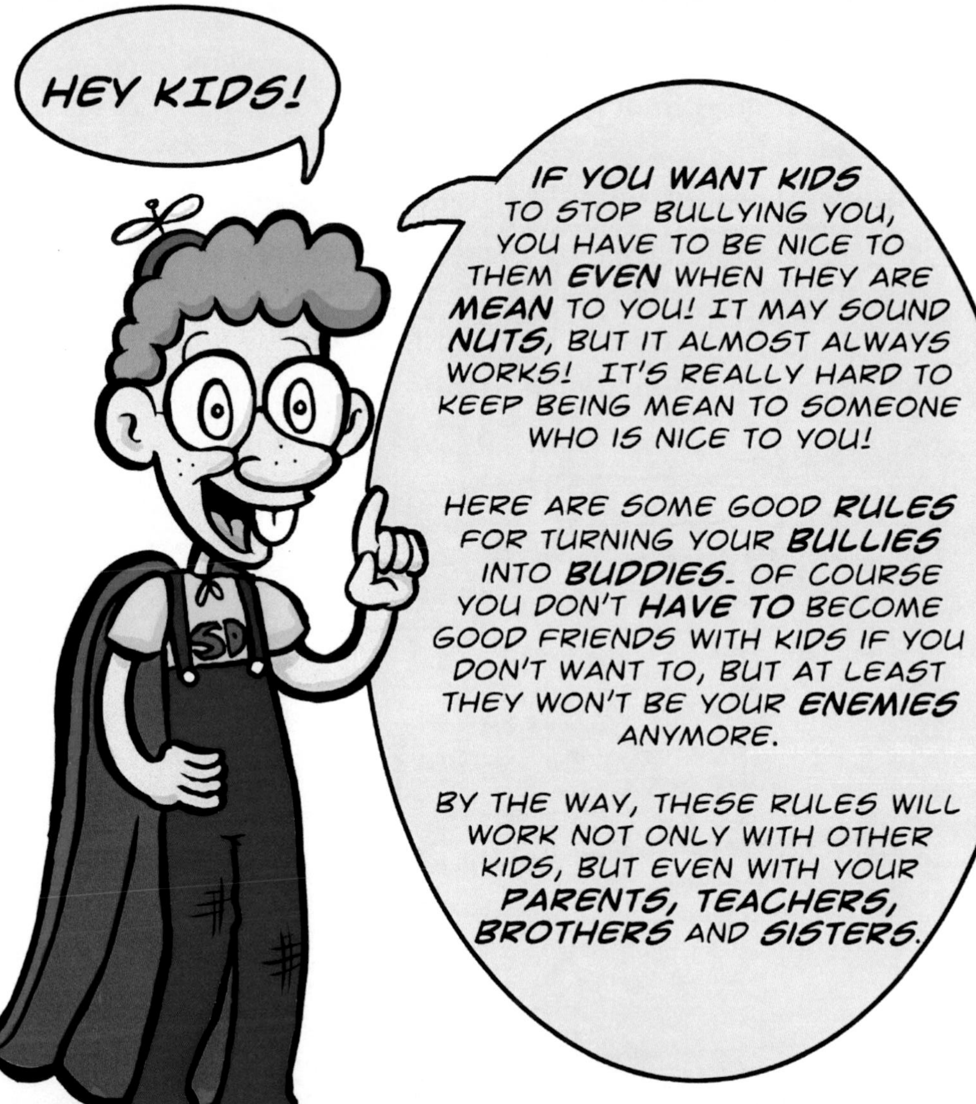

HEY KIDS!
IF YOU WANT KIDS TO STOP BULLYING YOU, YOU HAVE TO BE NICE TO THEM EVEN WHEN THEY ARE MEAN TO YOU! IT MAY SOUND NUTS, BUT IT ALMOST ALWAYS WORKS! IT'S REALLY HARD TO KEEP BEING MEAN TO SOMEONE WHO IS NICE TO YOU!
HERE ARE SOME GOOD RULES FOR TURNING YOUR BULLIES INTO BUDDIES. OF COURSE YOU DON'T HAVE TO BECOME GOOD FRIENDS WITH KIDS IF YOU DON'T WANT TO, BUT AT LEAST THEY WON'T BE YOUR ENEMIES ANYMORE.
BY THE WAY, THESE RULES WILL WORK NOT ONLY WITH OTHER KIDS, BUT EVEN WITH YOUR PARENTS, TEACHERS, BROTHERS AND SISTERS.
SD

Presenting the Bullies & Buddies™ rules.

BULLIES TO BUDDIES

RULE #1: DON'T GET ANGRY WHEN KIDS ARE MEAN TO YOU.

When we get angry at people, we *treat* them like enemies. So they treat us *back* like enemies.

Most of the times that kids pick on you, they are only doing it because they want to have fun seeing you get mad. It's like a game they are playing with you. If you get mad, you lose. If you don't get mad, they leave you alone and you come out being the winner.

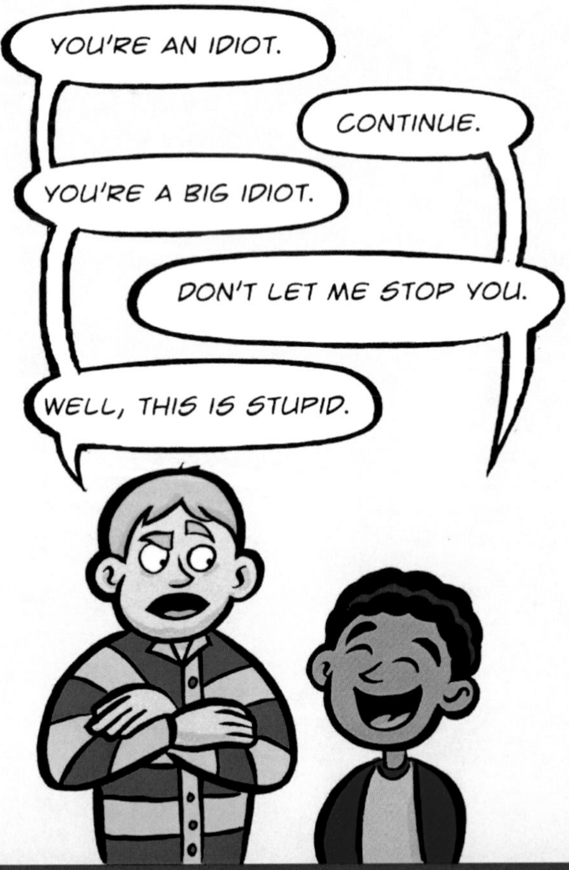
YOU'RE AN IDIOT.
CONTINUE.
YOU'RE A BIG IDIOT.
DON'T LET ME STOP YOU.
WELL, THIS IS STUPID.

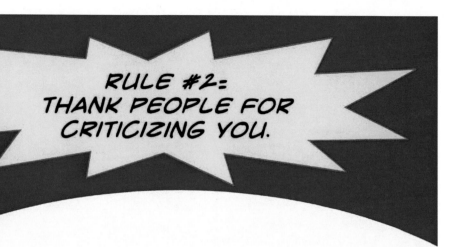

RULE #2: THANK PEOPLE FOR CRITICIZING YOU.

No one really likes to be told that there's something wrong with them. But tell yourself that when people criticize or insult you, it is really their way of trying to help you become a better person, even if they sound angry.

YOU'RE AN IDIOT.
THANK YOU. WHAT DO YOU THINK I CAN DO TO BECOME SMARTER?

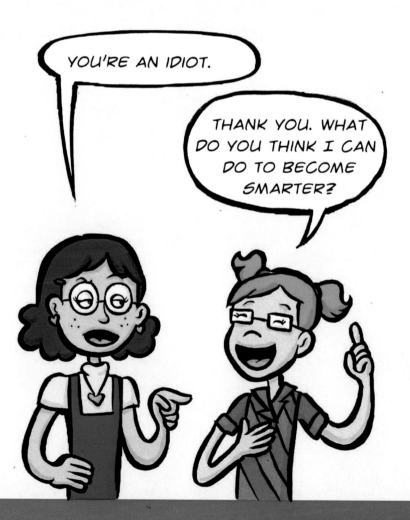

RULE #3: DON'T BE AFRAID OF PEOPLE

We fear *enemies*. So when we are afraid of people, we are *treating* them like enemies. Then they *respond to us* like enemies. Plus, we *lose* by being afraid, so they will *continute* to try to scare us.

Usually, when kids threaten you, they are just trying to scare you. So don't be afraid of them. If you treat them like friends, you won't *have* to be afraid of them because they won't *want* to hurt you. They may even want to *protect* you.

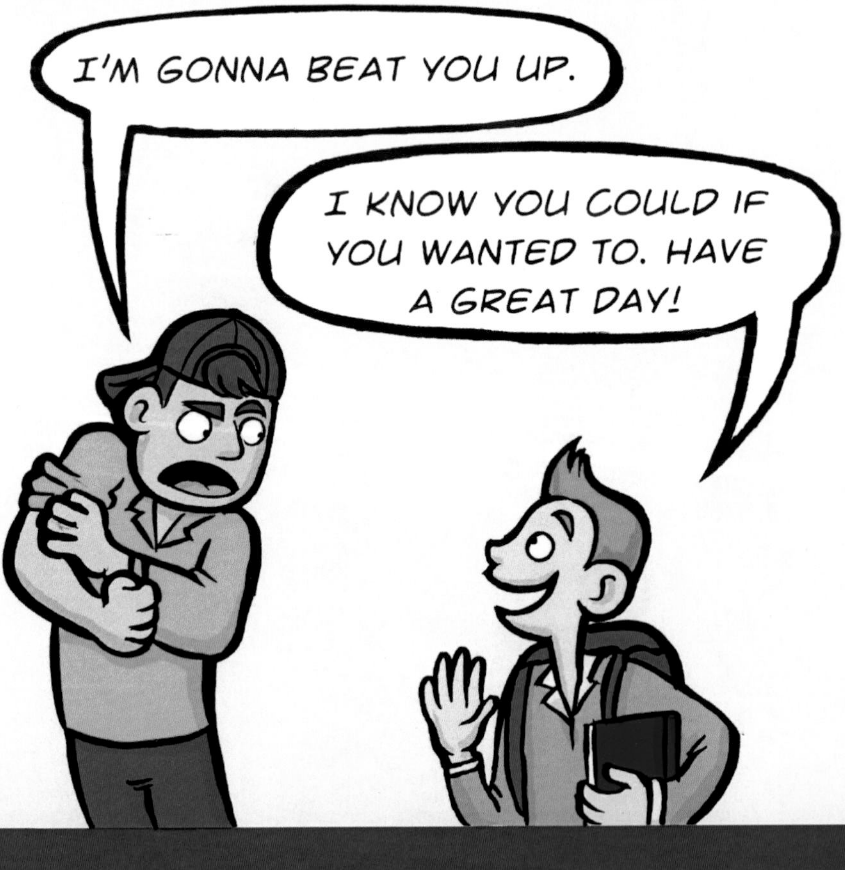
I'M GONNA BEAT YOU UP.
I KNOW YOU COULD IF YOU WANTED TO. HAVE A GREAT DAY!

RULE #4:
DON'T DEFEND YOURSELF

When we *defend* ourselves from people, we are *treating* them like enemies, so they will *continue* to attack us. If someone is truly trying to hurt your body, of course you should defend yourself if you can. But don't defend yourself when people are only trying to hurt your *feelings*.

I HEARD YOU CRY YOURSELF TO SLEEP EVERY NIGHT.

YOU CAN BELIEVE WHATEVER YOU LIKE. SEE YA LATER!

RULE #5: DON'T ATTACK PEOPLE.

When we *attack* people, we treat them like *enemies*. So even if kids attack you *first*, don't attack *back*. If they *insult* you, don't insult them back. And if they *hit* you, don't *hit* them back. When they hit you, you can ask, "Are you *mad* at me?" If they *aren't*, they will probably stop hitting you. And if they *are*, they will tell you why, and then you can talk to them about it. But they will no longer be hitting you.

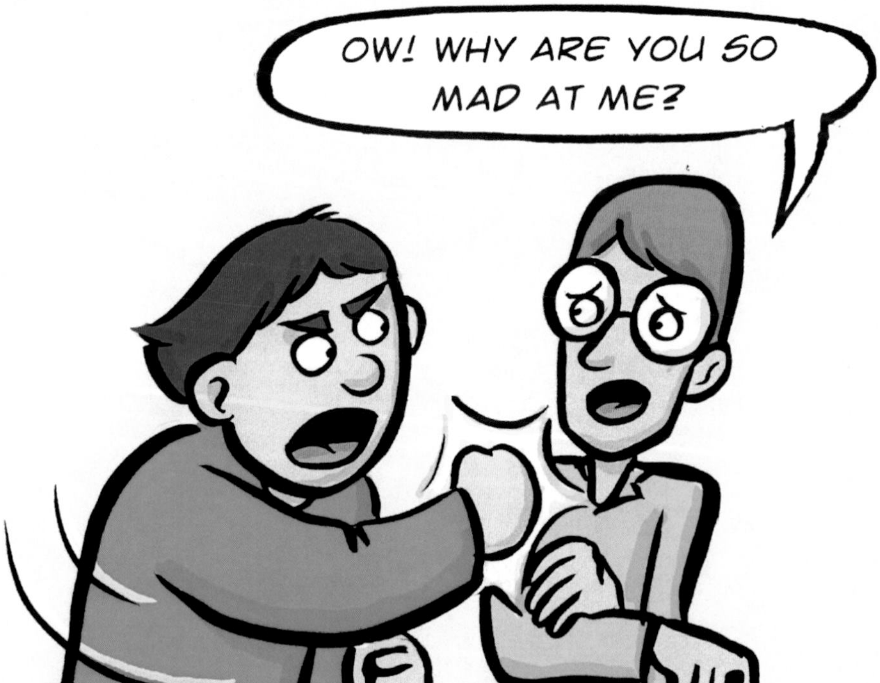

OW! WHY ARE YOU SO MAD AT ME?

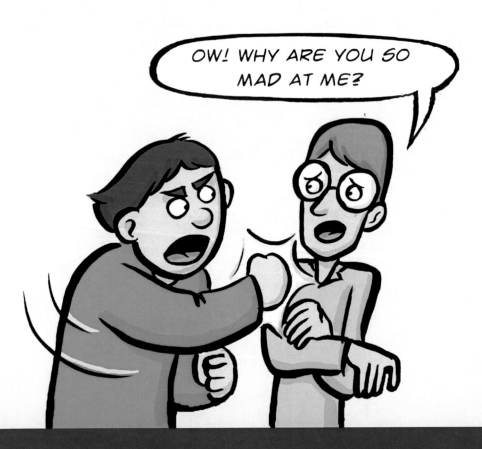

RULE #6:
IF SOMEONE HURTS YOU, LET THEM KNOW YOU ARE HURT, BUT DON'T GET ANGRY.

If we get angry when people hurt us, they get angry *back*. But if you just let them know how they *hurt* you, they usually feel bad and apologize.

If kids are saying mean things to you because they want to see you getting upset, then it is not a good idea to tell them they are hurting you. If you use Rule Number Two, the words won't hurt you because you will be thanking them for what they say. Only say they are hurting you when they are hurting your body or your important possesions.

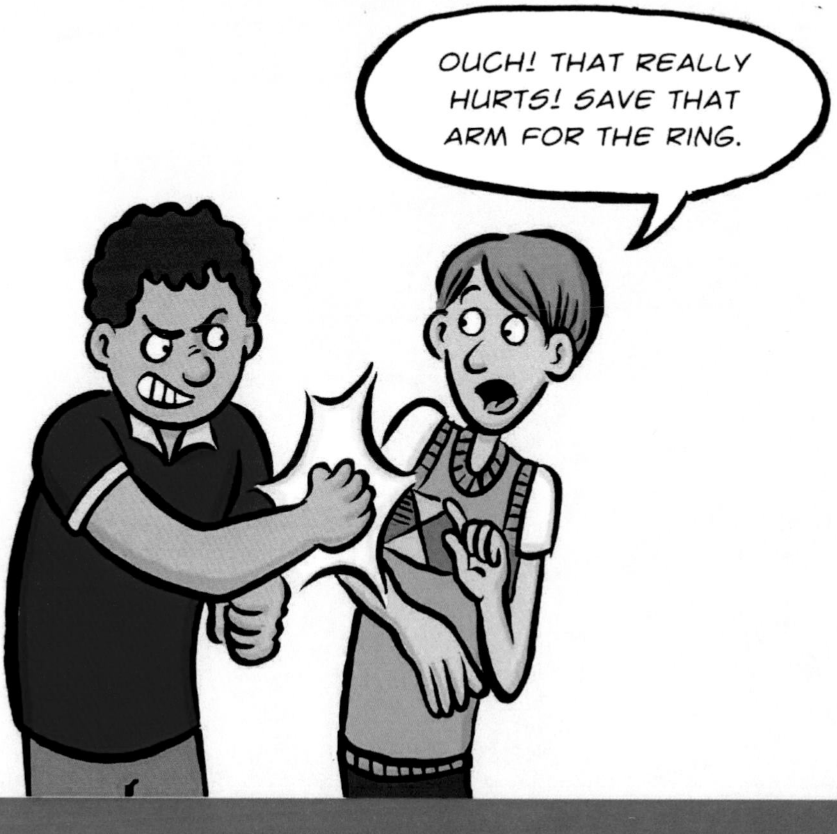
OUCH! THAT REALLY HURTS! SAVE THAT ARM FOR THE RING.

RULE #7: DON'T TELL ON OTHER KIDS.

Do you like it when kids *tell* on you? Of course not. Well, other kids don't like it when you tell on *them*. If they do something that upsets you, tell them *directly*. They will like and respect you much more than if you tell an adult on them.

Only tell an adult if someone has gotten hurt or to *stop* someone from getting hurt. It is also okay to tell an adult if you you want the adult to teach you how to solve a problem with other kids, but not because you want to get the kids in trouble.

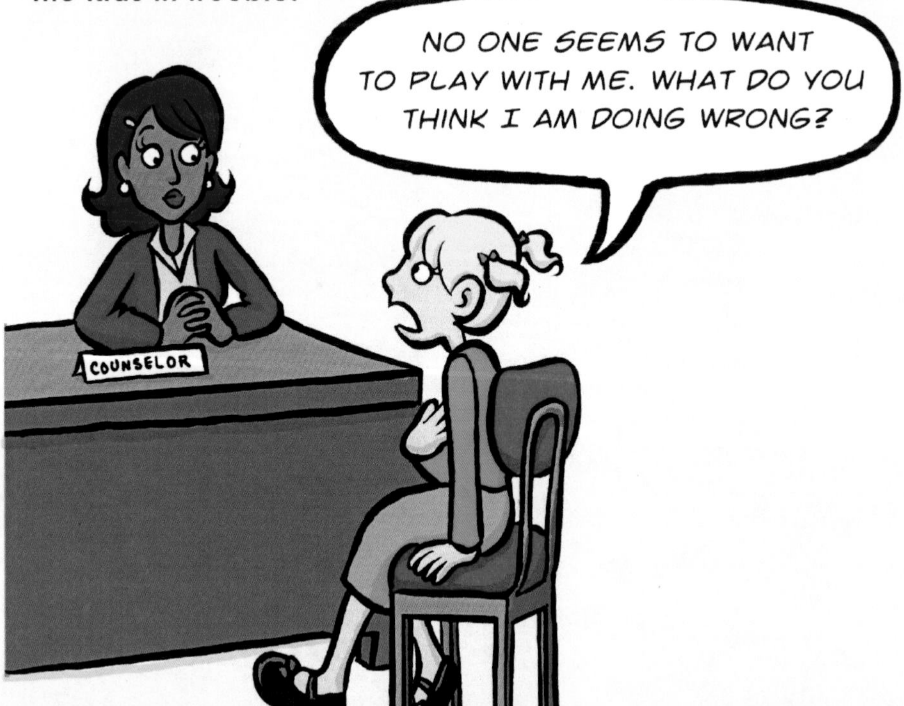
NO ONE SEEMS TO WANT TO PLAY WITH ME. WHAT DO YOU THINK I AM DOING WRONG?
COUNSELOR

RULE #8: DON'T BE A SORE LOSER.

No one wins all the time, and no one likes a sore loser. If we get *angry* when we lose a game, we look *foolish*. The other side may get angry *back*, and might not want to play with us any more. But if we *congratulate* them for winning, we make them feel good. They like and respect us better, and will be happy to play with us again.

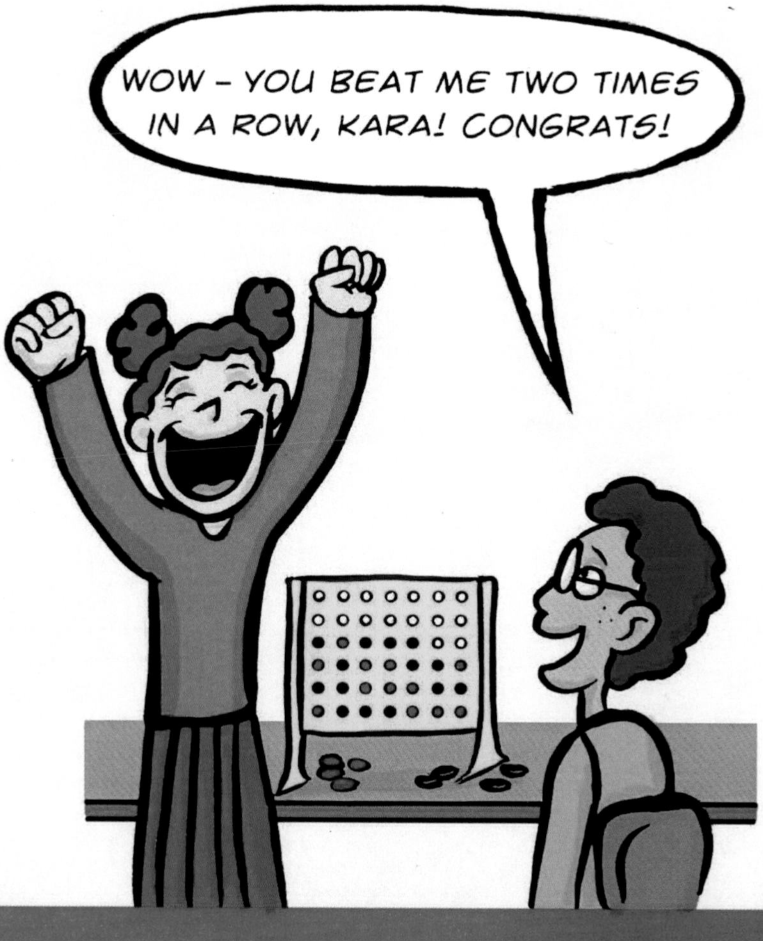
WOW – YOU BEAT ME TWO TIMES IN A ROW, KARA! CONGRATS!

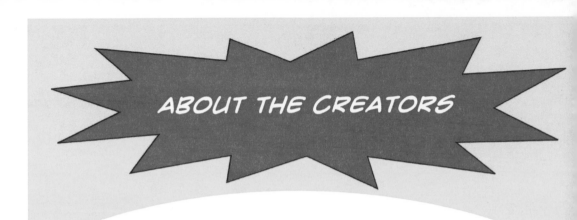

ABOUT THE CREATORS

IZZY KALMAN is a school psychologist and an expert in teaching people how to become winners by using the Golden Rule. He created the website www.Bullies2Buddies.com and produced other books and materials to help kids and schools solve the bullying problem. Izzy is also Lola Kalman's dad. He hopes Super-Dren will give you the super power of the Golden Rule to turn your enemies into friends!

LOLA KALMAN is a Cooper Union graduate, the producer of the *Bullies To Buddies™* video series and the illustrator of *How to Turn your Enemies into Friends*. She is addicted to art. Since she can remember, she has always had to quench her thirst for creativity by giving herself projects, like sewing pillows, writing books, sculpting clay, weaving bracelets and making videos. She encourages all kids to discover the world of art because whoever does will never be bored or lonely.

CHARI PERE is a freelance cartoonist from Staten Island, NY. Since graduating valedictorian from the School of Visual Arts in 2007, Chari has won numerous awards and fellowships. Her published works include MAD Magazine, The Girls' Guide to Guys' Stuff (Friends of Lulu, 2007), PresenTense Magazine, The Jerusalem Post, and LearningAboutDiabetes.org. You can view more of her work at www.charipere.com.

CHECK OUT MORE BULLIES TO BUDDIES PRODUCTS!

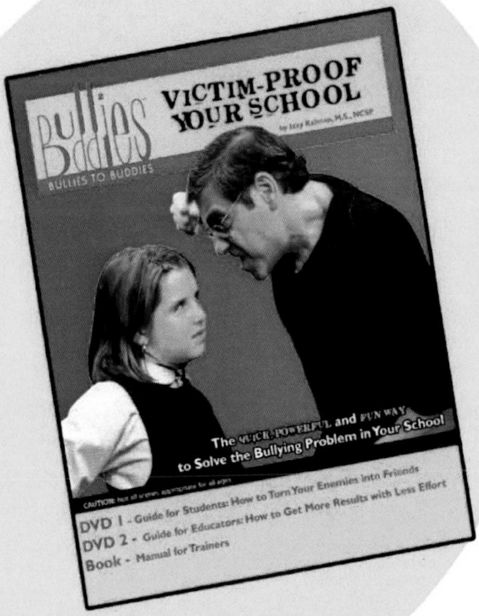
Bullies Buddies
VICTIM-PROOF YOUR SCHOOL
by Izzy Kalman, M.S., NCSP
BULLIES TO BUDDIES
The QUICK, POWERFUL and FUN WAY to Solve the Bullying Problem in Your School
CAUTION: Not all scenes appropriate for all ages
DVD 1 - Guide for Students: How to Turn Your Enemies into Friends
DVD 2 - Guide for Educators: How to Get More Results with Less Effort
Book - Manual for Trainers

PROGRAMS & TRAINING PACKAGES

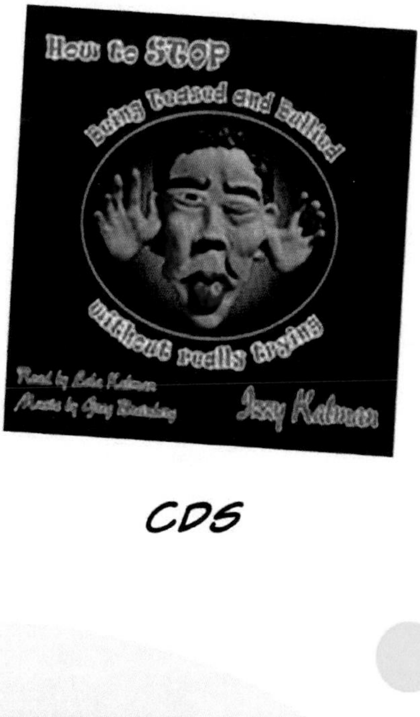
How to STOP
Being Teased and Bullied
without really trying
Izzy Kalman

CDS

BOOKS

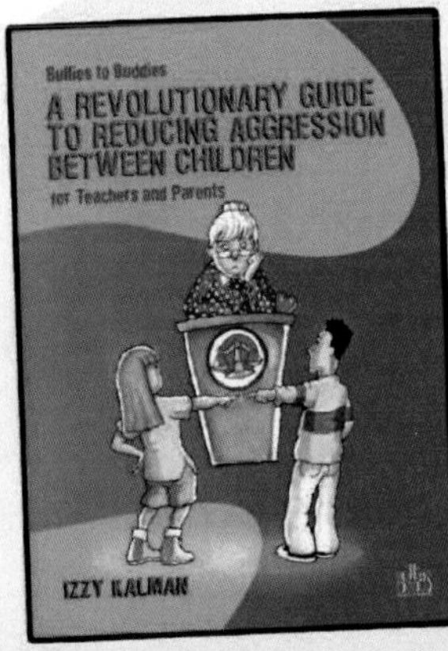
Bullies to Buddies
A REVOLUTIONARY GUIDE TO REDUCING AGGRESSION BETWEEN CHILDREN
for Teachers and Parents
IZZY KALMAN

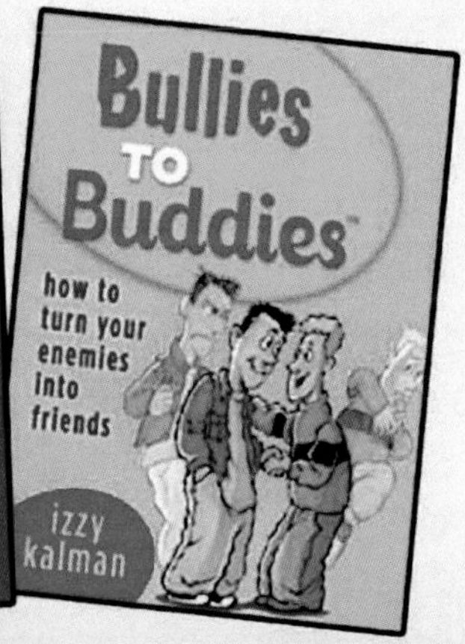
Bullies to Buddies
how to turn your enemies into friends
izzy kalman

...AND MORE!

WWW.BULLIES2BUDDIES.COM

What Professionals Say About Izzy Kalman's Bullies to Buddies Approach

"Finally, a program that works near miracles in helping victims to deal with bullies. After more than two years of implementing Izzy's principles, the students at William Snyder Elementary School smile at one another with confidence. Our school climate is pleasant and conducive to learning. Discipline referrals for bullying behaviors have decreased significantly. Teachers can now teach more because the kids are handling their own issues. And (drum roll here)...our test scores are going UP. In a school where the population is 63% Hispanic, our school reached every testing goal. In my 15 years as a school counselor, I have never seen a more effective social skills program. This one is pure genius." - *Jeannie Brewer, School Counselor, Snyder Elementary, Las Vegas, Nevada*

"We at PSI were so impressed with the simplicity and common sense of the Bullies to Buddies program that we had to make it our own. We have partnered with Izzy Kalman and Cleveland State University to bring this program to the thousands of students that PSI serves." - *Steve Rosenberg, PhD, Psychologist, President, PSI Solutions, Ohio*

"Of all the approaches to the problem of bullying, Izzy Kalman's approach stands out. It has worked wonders for my patients and friends alike." - *Doris M. Greenberg, MD, Developmental and Behavioral Pediatrician, Savannah, Georgia*

"Students are increasing their patience, compassion, and kindness towards other through applying your strategies. Our school is a better place because of Izzy's game! Thank you." - *Mark Lane, LCSW, School Social Worker, Guilderland Elementary School*

"This program has removed teachers from the middle of students' problems, no longer forcing them to choose who is right or wrong, and has helped students to regain control of situations and in turn their self esteem." - *Colleen Pittman, M.Ed, Coordinator/Counselor, St. Raphael School, Louisville, Kentucky*

Izzy Kalman is available for live school trainings, both in person and long distance by digital conference.

Substantial discounts are available for bulk purchases of Super-Dren and other Bullies to Buddies products.

For inquiries, send an email to contact@izzykalman.com *or call* **866-983-1333**